Leading Together

How Brave, Honest Conversations Can Transform our Lives, Organizations, and Communities

Steph Roy McCallum

Published by
Hybrid Global Publishing
333 E 14th Street
#3C
New York, NY 10003

Manufactured in the United States of America, or in the United Kingdom when distributed elsewhere.

McCallum, Steph Roy.
Leading Together
     ISBN: 978-1-957013-56-5
     eBook: 978-1-957013-57-2
     LCCN: *requested*

Cover design by: Natasha Clawson
Copyediting by: Dea Gunning
Interior design by: Suba Murugan
Author photo by: Hesh Hipp

www.bravelylead.com

Dedicated To

Ian, Rory, Caitlin, Griffin, and Ali who have taught me over and over again the power and beauty of connection and relationship that comes through brave, honest conversations.

To Meg, for your unconditional love and companionship.

Thank you all for being you.

Contents

PART 4 – Leadership in the Systems and Structures Around Us 157

Introduction

Deep breath. Begin.

The time has come. Really, it's long past due.

It's time for you and I to make choices that result in something different, and better, in ourselves, our organizations, and our communities.

Sometimes it's easier to start with all the things we know we don't want.

I know I'm tired of vitriol, blame, shame, and the divide between people.

I'm tired of name calling, cowardice, and self-indulgent behaviour that causes harm and diminishes others.

I'm tired of manipulation, hiding, and demonization of anyone and anything that isn't the same as you, no matter which side you are on.

I'm tired of people being so sure they are right that they can only make others wrong.

I'm tired of the aching despair that comes with witnessing people do and say brutal things to each other.

I'm tired of wishing there was more collaboration, compassion, and integrity in the public arena.

I know for certain that I want to stand for things, rather than against them. While it may be easier to identify what I don't want, I want to be part of building something better. I want action, movement, and the space between us to be full of curiosity, kindness, courage, and the rich ideas nurtured by our differences.

It's so easy to be against things, and so much harder to be for something; to build something up even when it's difficult and uncertain.

I want connection, deeper understanding, trust and strengthened relationships in the organizations I work in, in the family I am part of,

1

in the communities I live and work and play in so that we see, hear, and understand each other.

I want to build my capacity, and the capacity of others to lead with love, courage, compassion, and integrity. To lead our lives, organizations, and communities in this way so that we perform better, are more effective, creative, and innovative.

I want to be part of a movement that sparks a desire to see the humanity in each other, so we can heal our rifts, divides, and fractures, and so we can solve the complex difficult challenges we face.

I want to see leaders work together with those around them to make progress and achieve results, and find solutions to tough problems like climate change, systemic racism, inequality, and so much more.

I've learned through trial and error over almost three decades that those solutions are only possible when leaders lead in different ways, bringing people together to make changes, and that happens only when we trust and understand each other and are in a relationship. There is no checklist or to-do list that gets any of us to the solution without the hard work of talking together.

I come to this moment of deep yearning, ready for new action after decades of working in high emotion and conflict, watching leaders do the same things over and over again and none of it working. Leaders who demonize others, use fear to galvanize action, decide, announce, and defend their actions driven by ego and self-interest. Leaders who cause harm by maintaining the status quo that is unjust and inequitable, or who divide communities and create conflict in the wake of their interactions. Leaders who are focused on transaction; prioritizing tasks and to-do lists over people.

Watching the harm humans can do to each other has been a heart-breaking career, with precious moments of connection, understanding and compassion reminding me that there isn't much in the world that matters more.

I'm weary of the battle to find peace and understanding, yet at the same time uplifted by glimmers of hope, relationships, and the divide between people being crossed.

I want more of that.

I want more of that for all of us.

We learn at an early age what is OK to talk about in our families, and what we must avoid or stay away from. We learn if it is all right to talk about uncomfortable topics like sex, money, or the things that make us afraid or angry. We learn if harmony and sameness are valued and exalted, and if discord or difference are condemned and feared. We learn to behave according to those norms in order to survive or feel love and acceptance.

I learned at a very young age that harmony was prized above all else, and we were best to sweep difficult conversations and feelings under the rug, and then nail it down so nothing could seep out.

Those were the norms that the very good, kind people in my family set – probably norms that are similarly set in many families. We all do the very best we can, and there were countless positive things that came with the emphasis on harmony, sameness, and goodness. There were also lessons about hiding and avoiding and the fear that was palpable if we talked about hard things, we might break.

These are the strengths and the shadows that are within each of us, between us, and in the systems we are all part of. It's all there, and it is all necessary for wholeness to emerge.

The dictionary definition of wholeness refers to harmony, unity, and the state of being unbroken. Wholeness is about embracing the whole of what is within us, around us, and between us. Not avoiding, getting rid of, or compartmentalizing, but recognizing that we are all these things and so much more.

I have a friend who says that wholeness is being with the pain and the possibility at the same time. Wholeness is another word for integration, creating connections between different parts and linking them together where the whole is greater than the sum of its parts.

Wholeness is the foundation of well-being, individually and collectively in ourselves, in our organizations, and in society. Wholeness is also the foundation for performance, results, and outcomes. When we are whole, we are more productive, creative, and have access to everything within and around us.

I want wholeness for myself, for each of us, for our organizations and communities, and collectively.

There was one member of my family who was different from others, who taught me early on that it was good to disagree and to hold different opinions. My grandfather, Jim, was a petroleum engineer, and a staunch Texan Republican. He believed in hard work, helping others, pulling yourself up by your bootstraps, and carving your own path in the world. He believed in family, financial stewardship, and that each person has a place.

As a young woman I had passionate views on politics and the state of the world, views far different than my grandfather's. I spent many summers and holidays in my grandparents' house in Dallas, Texas, cooking and learning the art of gathering people together with my grandmother, and learning to disagree well with my grandfather.

My grandfather and I would sit together, and he would begin by asking a question, like what did I think about this news headline, or that story, or the state of the world in general? I would launch like a rocket with my views, passions, and intense certainty that the whole world needed to change to address wrongs or become fairer.

He would listen thoughtfully, often not looking me in the eye but staring out the window from his big Lazy Boy chair or looking at my grandmother's roses from his seat on the patio.

When I was done with my exertions he would say, "That's a pretty interesting perspective. Let me tell you a story."

He would speak slowly, with a Southern drawl, and invite me to listen to his views that painted the picture of another way to look at the same situation. He never asked me to agree with him. He never argued he was right, and I was wrong. He just listened and shared, and I shared and learned to listen.

Over time he came to call me the 'pinko' of the family, in affectionate tones. Merriam Webster defines 'pinko' as "a person who holds advanced liberal or moderately radical economic or political views." My grandfather meant it more like I was leaning towards communism rather than his own beliefs in republicanism, and it was always said with love and teasing.

Sometimes, when things would get emotional or heated, he would go silent. He would sit back in his chair and pull his pipe tobacco out and very slowly fill the bowl of his pipe, and then light it.

Once he had puffed a few times to get it going he would say, "It seems things are getting a little hot under the collar here. Let's think about this for a moment."

And then we'd both calm down, sitting in the swirl of pipe smoke, thinking our thoughts until we were ready to go at it again from a place of love and a strong relationship. We could agree to disagree, putting our relationship over any need to be right.

As we grow up, society enforces its own norms upon us; for example, that it is acceptable and expected for women to be empathetic and nurturing, but not for men. That it is acceptable and expected for men to be assertive and demonstrate anger, but not for women. Our communities and cultures invoke acceptable behaviours and attitudes of hierarchy, power, privilege, belonging, similarity, and what is suitable and what is not. Some of these norms we can see, and some lie beneath the surface.

At some point, we need to choose for ourselves how we want to be, what we value, and what we want to create in the world. In the end, that might be all we can control; how we show up and lead our lives, organizations, and communities. Whom we choose to be, especially in our darkest and most difficult moments, shines a light on the world we are building.

This is a book about the leader inside of you, inside of all of us, and what we choose to do with that potential of leadership to make a world for ourselves, each other, our children, and our communities.

I believe everyone has the potential to be a leader; to consciously choose the life they create and the contributions they make to creating good in the world. Leadership isn't determined by position, hierarchy, title, or attainment. Leadership is about the positive impact you have, what you stand for, and what you build in the world together with others.

This leadership book flows as follows:

- PART 1: Leadership begins with you
- PART 2: Leadership in the messy middle with others
- PART 3: Leadership in the space between us
- PART 4: Leadership in the systems and structures around us

More simply, I cover YOU, ME, US, and the SPACE of our most challenging conversations.

This is a book of stories and of lessons learned the hard way. This is a book of tender and difficult moments and insights about the power of connection that come from hard and important conversations in the face of high emotion and difficulty. I've shared some practices, some lessons, and a few questions for you to ask yourself as you read along.

I don't have all the answers, but I'm ready. Ready to learn from the past, to create a different future.

I think you are ready too.

This is less a "how to do this" book, and more an imagining of the world we might create if we sat in circles and had brave, honest conversations with each other when needed, even when they are hard.

If we can build our habits of talking together in this way, we can weave connections, deepen understanding, and strengthen trust and relationships. When those things are present, we can solve any challenge. When they aren't, we find ourselves lost in the world we live in now with sharp, polarized divides, intractable conflict, and winners and losers.

Let's choose change, together. Let's begin. Together.

PART 1

Leadership Begins with YOU

Part 1 is where everything falls apart, and I begin again, harvesting the lessons of failure, leveraging pain, grief, and heartache as a source of creativity and change. In Part 1, I come to realize that change begins with me, and with you, not with someone else.

For every leader in the public arena, the experience of standing in the fire of public controversy will be feared and familiar. This is the place where you grow--where crisis forges your character and creates commitments to be a better leader so you can solve problems together with others.

CHAPTER 1

Things Fall Apart

I've got nervous sweat trickling down my back under my sweater, and my palms are tingling. I feel slightly nauseous, just on the edge of an upset stomach and I can hear my own voice quaking and trembling as I speak.

My feet are solidly on the ground as I lean on the podium to respond into the microphone, and I'm glad I'm wearing flat shoes so my feet don't ache as the hours roll by with the questioning.

There is a part of me that keeps thinking, *Is this ever going to end?* but I keep batting that voice away to respond to another question.

Some of these people aren't even asking questions; more just voicing opinions and making statements about my general incompetence into their microphones so the video camera can catch their grand gesture. Some work themselves up and call me names with a question mark at the end, so they aren't called to order for a breach of the rules of procedure.

This isn't how it usually goes. I'm a facilitator – I ask the questions and other people have the answers. This time the conversation is about me, and it's being televised. My old mantra of leading high-heat conversations where I say inside my head, *"This isn't about me, this isn't about me, this isn't about me,"* so I can be grounded and present doesn't apply here. I don't have a replacement mantra to get me through this because this *is* all about me.

If this ever ends, I'm going to crawl into a small dark hole and hide for a month. Or maybe a year. I'm humiliated, embarrassed, and wholly to blame for the mess I find myself in. I believe that leaders take responsibility for their impact, and this has been a bitter, shameful thing to take responsibility for.

The Path That Led Me Here

Let me rewind a little.

I lead a consulting firm that designs, implements, and reports on conversations between communities and organizations about really hard issues, so change can happen.

I've been hired by this city to initiate a conversation with citizens about how they should spend the operating and capital budgets. That's a big, tough, messy, complex discussion with some wildly competing views. The city has a declining tax base, crumbling infrastructure, and some really, really tough decisions to be made about services that may need to be cut. They need the community to come to the table to understand and wrestle with these tough decisions and make recommendations on how to move forward.

My team and I spent nine months planning the process and designing the conversation; boiling the budget down into a workbook, creating online and tabletop games, designing workshops and deliberative forums, and training community groups to host their own conversations.

We've brought all our experience and expertise to this project, so people can grapple with the facts, understanding the budget as a tool to provide for quality of life and services that are valued. We know there will be multiple competing needs, opinions, and hopes in this process and we've planned conversations that create space for them.

Clearly that isn't going to happen now.

A Storm of Public Shame and Blame

As I stand at the podium being grilled by members of the city council, it's been one week since we publicly launched the project, after nine months of planning. I submitted my request to be a five-minute delegation at this special meeting of the council – a meeting called specifically to talk about the total public disaster of this project over the last week, and I lean on the podium answering questions for more than four hours, not five minutes.

In that one week the project website was launched…and then hacked and malware was installed, so we had to shut it down and begin the process of rebuilding a new site.

The online engagement tools were launched with questions about services that make a difference in people's lives…and then attacked and changed so citizens can only vote on options to fire me and my firm.

We launched a Twitter account and a Facebook page for the project… and social media has been on fire with stories accusing us of not knowing or caring about the citizens of this community, and any resident who tries to participate, share a view, or ask questions is shouted down in ALL CAPS by others telling them, "DON'T TALK TO THESE PEOPLE!!! THIS IS OUR COMMUNITY AND OUR CONVERSATION! DON'T ENGAGE. WE WANT THESE PEOPLE GONE. YOU ARE A LOSER AND A TRAITOR IF YOU TALK TO THEM."

We've closed the Twitter account and the Facebook page, so we aren't enabling a forum for some citizens to bully other citizens.

We created a Pinterest page where people could post pictures of what they want to see more of or less of in their community, and someone posted pictures of another community in another country by the same name, and a series of newspaper articles were written about my incompetence, as if I don't know where the community we are working with is located. We didn't post those pictures, but that doesn't matter now.

A hashtag has been trending nationally for six days, and the local, regional, and national media coverage has taken off like wildfire. It's become personal – directed away from the conversation and towards my company, and even about me personally.

We got 1.3 million tweets and retweets in the first twenty-four hours after we launched the project.

Let that sink in.

Nine months of planning and twenty-four hours to become a national sensation, and not in a good way.

It started with a simple question by one of my team members, clarifying an acronym a Twitter user had posted. That sparked a reaction where other Twitter users wondered who was behind the project's Twitter account, and a hashtag was born, and the piling on spread like wildfire. The main focus was to shut the conversation down — because we were from 'away' and the conversation should be led by someone local.

It went from an invitation to a conversation that matters to a total shit show in just days.

Nine months of planning, and just seven days of the public conversation and now I'm standing before the council to account for the giant mess that was meant to be a community discussion about the budget.

The project is co-branded; with the city's name and also the name of my consulting firm – meant to demonstrate that the city has brought in a neutral third party to lead these difficult conversations so there can be no claims of bias or concerns about integrity. Except now the conversation is totally about us and me personally, not about the project – specifically about getting rid of us and 'taking back' this conversation.

When the furor first erupted, our project partner, the city, suggested that some of the main Twitter users were known to them and the best course of action would be to be silent and that things would die down over a few days. Things didn't die down; they only escalated in intensity.

Taking Personal Responsibility for the Mess

Four days in we decided not to be silent – the conversation wasn't about the municipal budget anymore, it was about my firm and me and our perceived incompetence, lack of credibility, and the desire to replace us with someone local.

I decided to change course; I took out a full-page ad in the local newspaper and wrote an open letter to the citizens.

I apologized and took responsibility for all the mistakes and missteps in the process and I advocated for the conversation, encouraging people to participate in a discussion that would impact their community directly.

I wrote an open letter to the city council apologizing and taking responsibility for the challenges and encouraging them to stay the course – that the passion and intensity being demonstrated meant the conversation really matters.

After those letters ran, I was advised that the city council was calling a special meeting to discuss the project, and I should put in my request to be a five-minute delegation. Which is how I ended up standing at that podium sweating, shaking, and feeling like I might vomit.

When my grilling by the council finally concludes, I'm wrung out. Emotionally and physically spent. I've answered questions as openly and honestly as I can. I've taken responsibility for the countless mistakes and challenges in the project over the last week because while I didn't install malware, cyber bully citizens into silence, or post pictures of the wrong community on Pinterest, I am the one who designed the engagement process, so in the end I am responsible for what happens with the process. My job is the conversation, and the conversation is a mess, and even worse, people are talking about me, instead of the city budget.

After the televised city council meeting, Councillors gathered in a closed session to decide what to do about the contract with my firm. I got a phone call from the CAO the next day advising me that the council would like me to continue with the work I planned, and that they believe I am the right person to lead this difficult conversation. However, they would like to 'throw a bone' to the people who are outraged and ask that I do the project for half price. I'm shocked at the request but take a deep breath and let him know I will gather my team for a discussion and get back to him in a couple of days.

I gather the team in a hotel meeting room, as many of us in person as possible, with a few others on the phone. We do for ourselves what we do for a living; deliberate on the pros, cons, and consequences of making different choices to move forward. We work through as many impacts and outcomes as we can think of and we weigh doing the project, not doing the project, and modifying how we do the project and what our role might be.

In the end we decide that we are out, that we will not be involved in this process any longer. We've got two main reasons; 1) What does it say about the value of community engagement if it is suddenly possible at rock-bottom bargain-basement prices? We aren't overcharging the city — this is a project of more than a year, intended to allow the city to make really difficult decisions about operating and capital spending. It has, and will continue to take thousands of hours of our time. 2) The other reason we decide not to move forward is that we are no longer perceived as neutral. We can't be viewed as unbiased if the conversation is about us, and there is a worse danger that some people will choose not to participate in the conversation because it is my company or me leading the discussions, and that would exclude those voices. The integrity of the process has been impacted so we are no longer the right people.

I convey that message to the CAO. Over the following weeks we turn over all the materials, processes, and tools to the city. We conclude our contract, and the city pays us for our services to date. The CAO writes a glowing reference letter about me and our team, and I'm grateful for his thoughtfulness. I recognize there was probably some measure of guilt for how I have been publicly shamed motivating his choice of words, but I accept the letter with gratitude.

However, it doesn't end there.

The Ripples Continue

There is more to the fallout of this process than a few weeks of public shaming and blame. There is more to this story than the ending of a contract after some mistakes were made, and then moving on with business as usual.

For me, nothing is usual anymore.

I'm raw, shaken to my core, taken down to my knees, and find myself in a deep pit of shame. How did I think I knew what I was doing? Despite having spent over twenty years working in high-stakes situations, I must have just gotten lucky over the last two decades as it seems I have no idea how to handle a conflict. What am I capable of? What do I stand for? I know nothing for certain anymore. All the things I held to be true about how to work in the space of the public arena are up for question.

Perhaps all the brutal things said about me on the internet over the last few weeks are all true?

Up to this point, there is a mantra I've held while doing this work. *"This isn't about me. This isn't about me."*

I've thought this mantra allowed me to hold space for other people to bring their difficult emotions and challenges so I can help them navigate the conversation. It has grounded me and held me a little separate from those who are in the thick of the emotion. I've thought that distance and separation have made me a better facilitator. Except that mantra doesn't work here. Because this is all about me. I've been publicly shamed and blamed on a local, regional, and national stage. Some international colleagues have even taken note.

The fallout continues for months. The cancellation of this contract makes news among colleagues and clients, and a few other companies decide now is not the right time to work with me. They cancel contracts and projects as well. New work dries up; everyone is worried what it will mean to hire a firm or a managing director who has been humiliated on the public stage.

Colleagues come next; some people who have earned a living working as subcontractors for me over many years ask to disassociate themselves from my company, wanting to be removed from our website and taken off projects. Some of these people I had thought of as friends, and it cuts deeply to think they believe what has been said about me.

The blogs begin, with others assessing me and my handling of the situation, pointing out everything I've done wrong, and how they would have done things differently. It makes some big publications like PR news.

The public shaming continues, this time by my peers and colleagues.

Revenue declines and I begin to cancel the contracts of our temporary staff. Eventually, I lay off some full-time team members. I have to take out a mortgage on my house to keep the company running.

Some new work emerges slowly – interestingly, it often comes from clients who watched the public shaming and commend me for my authenticity, integrity, and courage as I navigated the challenges. Usually they've got really difficult, intractable challenges and they see that a dose of courage and authenticity might be what transforms the conflict they are experiencing.

None of these things is evident to me in the immediate months following the situation. I'm getting up each morning and managing the crisis, but mostly I'm just coping; focused on getting through the day, putting one foot in front of another.

Facing the Harsh Truth

I'm doing all the things that need doing but I can feel just under the surface that my heart is broken, my identity has been called into question, and I'm wandering lost in the woods. I ignore this as much as possible because I just need to get through the days, adapting our approach, managing the now smaller company, trying to harvest the learnings and lessons from this situation.

I realize that the work I do is part of who I am. Some people compartmentalize their work and their identity as separate. For me, working with high conflict and high emotion, and resolving big challenges has become my identity – I'm the woman who wades in and stands in the fire. Except that this time the fire consumed me, and when it died down, I wasn't sure who I was anymore. Everything I held to be true wasn't true.

I realize my mantra of "it's not about me" allowed me to hide in my work. Like hiding in plain sight, I could lead a challenging conversation but not need to put anything of myself out there.

I could be seen as brave, but not really need to be because I had nothing at stake.

I could be seen as openhearted or compassionate but not really need to be because my own pain wasn't in the conversation.

I could be seen as capable and credible, but I didn't have any answers, and what I stood for was just questions other people needed to answer. I could call them out to bare their souls and deepest stories, without needing to do so myself.

I could hide and not be seen because being fully seen is risky, scary, and dangerous.

I slowly begin to host what I call "Fail Fest" conversations, gathering people together to share their biggest mistakes and challenges so we can collectively learn from them. I share parts of this story; it's raw in the telling and often messy but the sharing of it starts to open the door to some lessons. It feels a bit like therapy and in some weird way it starts to connect me back to myself.

As a few years pass I stumble across this experience of mine written up in countless places; university text books for strategic communications, as a cautionary tale in a Canadian federal government guide for public consultation, blogs, and articles, and I even get word of a board meeting that puts the item on the agenda to discuss what they would do if that happened to them – all written up and discussed without my input or comment in varying degrees of accuracy.

The story has its own legs now, and the ground those legs stand on was a disaster of epic proportions.

I've got a small voice in my head that says *"I'm not enough. Not good enough, smart enough, capable enough, just not enough."*

Before this experience that voice was occasionally loud, but I could quiet it down. Since this experience, it has been hosting an epic party with a cast of thousands, affirming that it was right. Turns out I'm definitely not enough. Now I need to choose what to do with that knowledge.

I start to see that this work in the public arena requires something different.

Seeking a New Way

Being unbiased and neutral isn't the answer, and it also isn't true. We are all biased and view the world through our own lens and experiences, so suggesting we are neutral is a lie that means we don't need to fully show up.

I start to see that these hardest of conversations in the public arena take a new kind of leadership; leaders who show up, take a stand, and have the heart to stay when things get really messy.

I start to see that hiding or standing behind a role, position, or emotional armour separates us from each other and contributes to how easy it can be to blame, shame, and demonize others. That means the antidote might be found in authenticity, integrity, and bringing my own humanity to conversations in the public arena. So much easier said than done, and such a vulnerable, scary thing to contemplate.

As I unravel the personal, emotional, and identity effects on my life, I begin to wonder what it might look like if the world was full of leaders who chose courage and compassion over blame and shame. Those who did the right thing even when it was hard, who brought people together rather than pulled them apart. I wonder what kind of leadership that is, and where to find it. How did I find it in myself and in others?

I knew I didn't have the answers, but it was time to go looking for them.

How we were interacting with each other, the ease with which people's lives and communities were taken apart and dismantled with little thought to consequence, the impacts on people's hearts and souls were being felt everywhere as society splinters and polarizes further into camps and factions.

This horrible, awful, painful experience I'd just been through was turning out to be a hard-won gift, a lifetime of lessons in a few short months.

Here is one of the few things I know for certain: that if you are going to talk about important things with other people there will be times that you will fail.

If you are going to do it publicly, that failure might be witnessed by others.

If you are going to bring people together to discuss tough topics in an environment where blame, shame, vitriol, and an intolerance for imperfection is the norm, then you might feel the pressure and unease of mistakes and missteps.

Here is another thing I know for certain: that when you stand fully in failure, when you call in the tendency towards blame, shame, and perfectionism, when you show up authentically in service to deepening understanding, you can change the environment where you are talking about the most difficult of things, if even just for a few moments.

When we do that, we shift the conversation to explore our full humanity, and that just might be an antidote to polarization and a deep divide. The place to start is in welcoming failure as a path to learning and growth.

The Challenges and Gifts of Failure

Failure is life's way of growing you. If you can stay long enough with the pain, heartache, and shame failure gives you, learning will emerge.

Most people wish for the easiest, simplest path to resolution — the path with the fewest bumps, least discomfort and the 'life hacks' laid out in a checklist. I wish that for all of us too. However, I'm learning instead that there is no easy path to learning lessons, working things out, and making things better when everything has gone sideways. It's really easy to call it a 'fail fest' and it's really hard to be in the moment of failure, staring in the mirror at the sickening realization that you aren't what or who you thought you were and that you've let yourself and others down.

There are a few things I've come to realize about learning from failure. Maybe they will help you begin to think differently about the messy, chaotic, charged space we live in, and how to learn from and lead in all the moments when you don't get things right.

- **Failure will strip you naked and have you run down a crowded street on your own.**
  That sounds like a nightmare, and it is. There is no 'fun' in failure. It is deeply painful, often full of shame and fear and even grief. It cuts you off at your knees and exposes you to the world. It makes you want to hide, makes your pulse race, keeps you up night after night. I'm speaking from experience. If you haven't felt these things, then the failure probably wasn't yours. Maybe you made a mistake or a misstep, but you didn't fail — there is a distinct difference in terms of impact and scale that distinguishes mistakes from failure. It strikes me that if you can quickly and smoothly talk about learnings and fail fests then you probably made a mistake rather than failed.
- **There are deeply painful, usually complicated, multifaceted stories that go with failure. To tell those stories with integrity, they must be yours to tell.**

I often say in my workshops on brave, honest conversations that when we leave this discussion you should take your own stories with you and leave the stories of others behind in this room; we won't repeat other's stories when we leave. In some sectors there has been a focus on 'collecting stories' to bring lived experience to life; stories of indigenous people; stories of immigrants and refugees; stories of patients in the health care system.

When you take someone else's story and retell it for emotional impact you take something precious away from someone else. You can't dress up someone else's story and call the learning your own— it lacks integrity and authenticity and becomes performance rather than learning or ownership of failure. You have to own your really hard, painful, difficult story in order to find the lessons in it, and no one else can do this for you.

- **You have to sink into failure to learn from it, and you have to go through the trench to get to the other side.**
When you have failed, especially if it is a major failure, it can feel like a disaster. It makes you question everything about who you are, what you stand for, your credibility, capacity, and abilities. It can make you question your whole life. It hurts physically, emotionally, and intellectually. The beauty and the horror of it is that there is this requirement to experience pain as the path to knowledge. You cannot get there without really feeling the feelings. There is no life hack, checklist, or step-by-step guide to finding the lessons or getting out of failure faster. There can be deep, transformative learning in failure, but the path to that place is hard and treacherous.

- **You are going to fail.**
If you can let go of your drive to get things perfect or exactly right and be open about getting it wrong when you fail, then it is possible your recovery will be faster. You will have more self-acceptance and be quicker to take ownership of the failure. That will move you from the emotional wasteland of initial failure to recovery and learning.

Many are talking about running towards failure in order to innovate — and the truth is that trying, testing, creating, iterating, and adapting are all steps to true innovation. Organizations and individuals who fail, recover, and get up and do it again are the ones who succeed. That is one of the gifts of failure.

We don't see a lot of that in the public arena, but we could see it if you and I started modeling and making it OK to mess up, recover, and learn together with others. If we give ourselves permission, we also give others permission to fail, and that can change all sorts of dynamics between people.

- **Your failure is your opportunity and your growing edge.**
  If you can take ownership of your failings with deep humility and self-awareness, you will find the path out. If you don't own the failure and your role in it with humility and self-awareness there will be few lessons for you. You will be more likely to smooth it all over, dress it up and put a bow on it, choosing armour or a persona to step into.

  Failure gives us a window into transformation. It asks much of us and in return it gives back growth, knowledge, and learning. You will be a better leader because of your failure. Failure changes you — often for the better.

That's my list of how to really learn from failure. No checklists, life hacks, or easy solutions. There is no easy way through it. Failure sucks, and failure is a gift. Both of those things are true.

Reflect and Practice – When You Fail and Falter

Reflect on the situations, events, and moments in your life that have been hardest and most challenging for you.

- How can you sink into and be fully present to the challenges and lessons of these situations?
- How can you build your capacity to be with the discomfort of looking into your failure?
- What growth and learning are there for you? How might it stretch and expand your skills, knowledge, and ways of being?
- How will you choose to step into the gift of failure the next time it comes knocking at your door?

You are going to get things wrong. You are going to fail in life and work. Knowing that, you can choose to harvest the insights from the challenges, practicing forgiveness for yourself and others.

When you choose learning and growth, your conversations with others hold the potential to be different, and that's a good thing. That different way is a first step on the road to positive momentum in your life, organization, and community.

CHAPTER 2

Owning Your Strengths and Your Shadows

I have run my own consulting firm for fifteen years, and been working in high-stakes, high-conflict situations for more than twenty years. I've got a background in authentic leadership, community development, and conflict resolution. I've worked on five continents, across cultures, stepping into challenging situations to bring people a little closer to each other, to find a way forward.

My experience reads like a résumé, and I say that because it holds the *"I'm not enough"* voice at bay just a little and reminds me that I might have it within myself to summon the courage to be of service. It doesn't really work to build my confidence, but it can mask it enough to let me slide through the uncertainty.

My epic failure on the public stage has made this hole in my heart a little bigger and I'm struggling with how to reconcile it. I've been pulling apart my practice and career, unraveling years of assumptions and what I hold to be true.

Looking for Answers

I turned to coach training in an effort to seek the skills needed to support others. And once I'd become a coach, I wondered if we built up the capacity of each individual in a difficult conversation to be self-aware, mindful, open to possibility, and heart-centered, would it channel our better angels productively when we engage with each other or when things get difficult?

I think I'm searching to find that for myself as I recover and recreate what I stand for, what I believe in, and what I want in the world in the space between us.

If I'm brutally honest, I'm not really searching for the antidote to polarization for others. I'm searching for myself. Isn't it true that if I yearn for something, it is possible that others do too?

I completed coach training and added leadership coach to my résumé. It brings me a little closer to my own heart, and it brings me home to myself.

I begin to realize that coaching isn't going to be the antidote to polarization in the public arena that I had hoped it might be, instead it's just another piece of the puzzle in human interaction.

Coaching may help me contribute to closing the divide by supporting others to develop their capacity to lead, but I'm looking for something else, something outside of me, that will give me the magic answer so I can go and apply it in the public arena and (hopefully, deeply wishing) that it will be a catalyst for something different.

That's what I'm yearning for – something different. There must be a different way to cross the widening space between people in the public arena.

Brave, Honest Conversations About Your Impact as a Leader

At the moment of this story, I find myself seven months into a ten-month-deep leadership-intensive program with a group of leaders from around the globe. I'm sitting in the woods in the hills of North Carolina, messy crying, and sobbing, feeling my heart break into little pieces in front of this group as I receive their feedback.

There are twenty-four of us in this leadership program, and we've been supporting, encouraging, calling each other out and onward, and occasionally pushing each other's buttons for more than half a year.

We are sitting in the community room, with its wood-panelled walls and cozy cushions. We've designed this session ourselves, with some guidance from the program leaders – our goal is to give each other feedback that grows each of us as a leader. We've set some ground rules:

- One leader in the spotlight at a time, and that leader decides the order and pace of receiving feedback.
- Everyone offers their feedback from a place of love with a goal of growing that person – so check with yourself if what you are offering is coming from that place, and if it isn't don't offer it.
- There is no piling on – once something has been said, don't offer it again.
- Someone in the group will take notes for the leader in the spotlight so they can be fully present to the moment and not have to worry about remembering everything.
- Be real with our feedback (versus being nice, gentle, or easy).

We've turned the lights low, so that those offering feedback sit in shadow, sprawled around the room in various positions on the floor.

The leader in the spotlight sits in an alcove with a window seat and cushions and a light shining on them.

We've drawn names to indicate the order of who is in the spotlight and when. It's a little theatrical and there are equal parts of love and fear in the room. Our hope is to set the stage for a profound and memorable growth experience, but we are all aware everything could shift and become a *Lord of the Flies* experience quite quickly if we aren't careful.

Now it's my turn in the spotlight. Feedback is offered in three categories:

- You succeed as a leader when…
- You have an unintended impact as a leader when…
- You fail as a leader when…

I choose to receive feedback in the order listed because I know that what I will focus on is the feedback related to failure. Perhaps starting with success will allow some of it to sink in.

Embracing Strengths and Shadows

Here is the feedback I was offered.

I succeed as a leader WHEN:

- All the time.
- I relax and trust those around me.
- I lead with vulnerability.
- I give space to others.
- I challenge the rules.
- I dream big.
- I let go of structure and let things unfold.
- I ask for help.
- I lead from the heart.
- I don't hold back.
- I lean into my fierce commitment to grow others and have a positive impact.
- I lead from conviction and also curiosity.

I have an unintended (positive or negative) impact as a leader WHEN:

- I follow my willingness, and comfort and desire to take others down an uncomfortable path (positive).
- I lead with a depth of strength and faith in others (*"I would go to war with you."*) (positive)
- I show others how not to be afraid of messy, sticky conversations. (positive)
- I create space for risk-taking, bravery, and doing hard stuff together. (positive)
- I think I know the solution without waiting for others to see it. (negative)
- I take a stand for inclusivity that welcomes everyone in. (positive)

I fail as a leader WHEN:

- I give in to frustration.
- I think I am speaking for others but I'm really only speaking for myself.
- I talk strategy but I'm really speaking about my emotions cloaked in strategy.
- I choose to always lead from the front, rather than recognizing that leading from the side or behind can be just as impactful.
- I believe I am the only one who understands the answers or approach needed.
- I lead with boldness and courage alone, rather than boldness and courage grounded in love and compassion.
- I'm so strong in what I think that other people can't find their voice.

Even writing this feedback on the page gives me a trembling feeling of nausea. It is powerful and life changing to be fully seen, and also a deeply vulnerable experience.

I have come to realize that my work in conflict transformation has allowed me to create the illusion of being seen in front of the room while being fully hidden. When the conflict isn't yours, you don't need to be vulnerable or open. I have to come to realize that my biggest fear is being fully seen. Hiding makes me less effective, less authentic, and I have less positive impact in the most difficult of conversations. When I show up fully human, others do too, as they are called out to show themselves by my humanity. It's human nature – we mirror the ways in which others interact with us.

Leadership and life are an ongoing balancing act, a dance between poles, holding to the middle and acknowledging the pull to one side or another. Leadership and life require you to show up as your full, authentic self, leaning into your strengths and gifts, welcoming your flaws, mistakes, and weaknesses as dear old friends, and building your awareness so you can make conscious choices from a place of commitment to something outside yourself. When we lead from a place of wholeness, anything is possible.

That's what I'm yearning for; leaders who lead their lives, organizations, and communities in ways that call us in, leaders who bring their whole selves to their commitment to make change.

You Are All These Things and so Much More

When people say you have acted or shown up in ways that are opposite or different from what you value, or your strengths, it can create a real struggle. It can hurt, make you feel bad about yourself, and may also make you question your leadership. Sometimes the things people say are more about them than about you, but that doesn't mean what is said is not hard to hear.

Leadership in this space of brave, honest conversations requires you to embrace all of your strengths – and also all of the shadows of those strengths.

The act of acknowledging you have strengths and also shadows acts as a counter to a world where conversations are fraught with saying the 'right' thing, or being on the 'right' side, instead of welcoming the humanity we each bring with compassion and courage.

I think of this as 'we are all these things and so much more.' Shadows are not the opposite of our strengths, instead they are like the dark underbelly of those strengths, where we lean in too far without balance or integration. They are sometimes the parts of ourselves we see in others and dislike. They are within us, and if we raise our awareness of them, we can work with them. If we ignore or avoid them, they can do us and others harm and our impact will be less. For example:

- You can be kind, and also be the shadow of kindness, which is sickly sweet and disingenuous.
- You can be lighthearted and playful and the shadow of that which is irresponsible and focused on personal pleasure and desire over the needs of others.
- You can be grateful and also its shadow, which is needy and clinging.
- You can be empathetic and caring, and also its shadow where you have few boundaries and low self-care, leaning into self-sacrifice.

- You can be humble, and also its shadow of self-doubting.
- You can be bold, and also step into the shadow of arrogance.

All of this is part of being fully human.

Great leadership is fully human leadership.

If you only accept the "positive" parts of yourself, you are only creating space for half of what is in you, judging, rejecting, or ignoring the rest.

When we do that for ourselves, we tend to do that with others too – contributing to intolerance, blame, shame, and a need for perfection in our relationships, organizations, and conversations.

Reflect and Practice – Your Strengths and Shadows

If you can be with your strengths and your shadows, you can be with other people's strengths and shadows too. If you can only be with your strengths, there is only space to be with other's strengths, and no allowances for their shadows. We perform better, are more effective, and have stronger relationships when we have access to all that is within us, and within others.

Consider:

- How do you separate the things that are yours and the things that are someone else's?
- How do you love the shadow parts of yourself rather than reject them?
- How can you look at all the things that you are with a loving heart and self-compassion?
- What do you see when you slide from strength to the edge of a shadow, and what are the signs that you are slipping?

The act of growing in leadership is not that you always do it perfectly, or that you are always meeting every challenging situation with loving kindness. It is that you have a deep awareness of the whole of you, and an ability to accept and integrate that whole, messy human that you are and lead from authenticity. When you do that, you can accept the whole, messy human across from you, and that is the first step to having brave, honest conversations.

Here are some questions to explore for yourself as you deepen your thinking about how you show up and interact with others.

1. What are the behaviours, actions, and mindsets you see in others that create a reaction in you?
2. Where are those things in you? How and when do they show up?
3. What are the shadows to each of your strengths?
4. How might you look deeply at those shadows and welcome them with love and kindness?
5. How might you build your awareness of when you move from strength to shadow? What conditions or situations create that possibility?

Growing your leadership for brave, honest conversations begins with you. What do you stand for? What are you committed to? What impact do you want to have? How comfortable are you with your own strengths and shadows? The greater your comfort with your own, the greater space you can make for others.

There is no destination in leadership development. There is always growing to do, as we are always a work in progress, and stretching the boundaries of your own growing edges.

Leadership is not about a role, position, or hierarchy. It is about making conscious choices to authentically lead in your life, organization, and community based on your commitment to creating something in the world, to engaging, inspiring, and empowering others to create the world they yearn for too.

CHAPTER 3

What Are You Committed to Growing in Your World?

For two years after the situation that led to my national public shaming, I struggled to find solid ground under my feet. It's not that I was depressed; it's more that I was questioning everything I thought I knew, wandering without a map, seeking answers on how to heal myself and the polarized, reactive world that had resulted in me being the focus of public controversy.

What I wanted in my secret heart was to shut down my business, and to take the time to rethink the recipe for building public trust in a time of public outrage.

I wanted to sink into other ways of working that didn't involve taking on a public conversation for another controversial project, managing the emotion, and then writing the report on the next steps. It all felt so transactional, so useless, so lacking in making impactful change. I wanted to create real deep connection between people in conflict so they could see and hear each other's humanity, so the people and the conversation would be different when it was done. I wanted to be part of transforming the most difficult situations, of building relationships and trust where there was none, of making some small difference in the face of impossible challenges.

I was coming to understand that these outcomes would require more than the traditional work of planning a public engagement process,

31

facilitating some conversations, and writing up the results. It would require capacity building in communities and inside organizations for different ways of being and interacting. It would take leadership development for a different way of working and approaching complex conversations, and it would take an entirely different focus for our conversations if we wanted long-term systemic change.

I didn't think I could sink into the kind of thinking required to create new ways of working at the same time I continued to run my company; doing business development, taking on projects to pay salaries and the bills, mentoring and coaching staff, and doing work I straight out had no more energy for.

What Do You Really Want in the World?

It took two years of discussion with my husband to help him understand the depths of my unhappiness and restlessness doing what I had always done and denying this other way of working that was calling me.

It was so hard to admit to myself that this business I'd built, and that had survived a major catastrophe, and that had been my identity for decades, was now a place of work where I was lost, where my heart was just not in it any longer. I was afraid too. Walking away would mean starting again, and that meant financial and professional risk. Plus, I wasn't entirely sure what I was going to create instead, but all I could think about was that I knew I needed time to figure it out.

The desire to walk away was so deep it was all I could hear some days that included a mantra of *"I want out"* repeating itself over and over again in my head. I was a little desperate about it – to be free, to have space and time, to recover, heal, and reinvent myself and my work. It felt as alluring as an escape to a South Pacific island. I could feel a tangible pull to run away, and to run toward something I couldn't yet see. Have you been there? Can you feel that pull? When the call to get out, leave, end things, and relieve your suffering becomes so loud that it is all you can hear?

Perhaps it was my version of a midlife crisis, but instead of buying a convertible or having an affair I was yearning for meaningful, purposeful change.

I decided to close the business and begin again.

I needed to tell staff that the business would be closing, and to give them lots of time to make new plans. This made me nervous and anxious, but it also felt so real, and like such an important step in the right direction. It was early spring, and I thought letting people know that when the summer began, and we would be closing our doors it would provide lots of time and salary for my team to transition to whatever was next for them.

I was in Halifax, Canada, delivering training with one of the senior consultants, so I decided to break the news to her over dinner. We sat down in one of the many lovely restaurants in that city and ordered glasses of red wine while we looked over the menu. I was nervous; it's hard to give someone notice and it's just as hard to tell them you are ending their job because you want something different, and that you aren't even sure what that is.

There were parts of me that felt guilty, like I was making choices to put myself ahead of others and that wasn't all right – it was selfish. I took a deep breath and shared my journey over the last couple of years; the depths of my despair in doing work that no longer called to me, and the uneasy feeling that in doing the work in traditional ways I was contributing in some small way to the state of distrust and polarization in the public arena, and how my own ethics and values were so out of alignment with that possibility. I shared my seeking and yearning for something different, and for a new way of working, and even though I hadn't quite figured out what that new thing looked like I was going to take a big leap and close the business so I could figure it out. I shared my desperation and how loud the call was to change direction in my career. I shared my sadness at ending the chapter of my company, and my worry and hope that she had enough time to make the transition for herself.

She responded with grace and understanding. She said she'd known I was struggling, and it made sense after everything I'd been through. She was appreciative of the long lead time to transition to a new job. I can imagine she was also worried and anxious about the changes in her life, but they hadn't surfaced for her yet.

Then she surprised me. She asked if I'd thought of taking on a partner who could run the business and keep the company operating, while

I focused most of my attention on figuring out this new thing. She wondered if she might be that partner. It was an option that had never occurred to me, and I agreed that it deserved some thinking through.

Sometimes You Make the Wrong Decision for the Right Reason

You know when you look back on a moment in your life and you see with hindsight that the decision you made for all the right reasons was still a bad decision? When you look back and can see you made a decision because you thought you SHOULD do it, not because your heart was telling you it was right? In fact, perhaps your heart was telling you that you should definitely NOT make that decision, but you overruled it?

This was that decision for me.

I talked it over with my husband, my coach, and colleagues. Most everyone agreed it made sense, that it was a rational, common-sense decision, that it kept income and revenue flowing for multiple people and it solved my problem of wanting to work on other things. Everyone thought it was fine to take on a partner and keep the company going with business as usual while I explored some new ideas -but no one was excited for me or enthusiastic about the idea. No one was jumping up and down cheering me on – except my colleague who suggested she become my partner. She was excited. I wasn't excited at all, and I felt guilty about not feeling good about the choice. I felt trapped and coerced into doing what other people wanted instead of what I was yearning for, or what seemed like the 'right thing' to do, even when it didn't feel right to me. I also felt bad about feeling bad about what seemed like a perfectly reasonable decision. The feelings had little to do with my colleague – she was and is a smart, capable, thoughtful woman. She was excited to stretch and grow her own skills, knowledge, and capacity and to learn how to run a company.

I chose to move forward, and we became partners.

I worked hard to choose a perspective that this was a great opportunity, a new beginning, and that it would be wonderful to have a fellow collaborator and partner. There was a lot of self-talk, motivating, bullying, and encouraging myself into the 'right' mindset each day. Some days I was successful, and other days I was lost, resentful, frustrated, and yearning to leave.

I tried that for two years.

Wrong Decisions Have Consequences

In those two years I felt like I was slowly dying and losing my sense of purpose. Two years where my creativity disappeared, my commitment and satisfaction from the work was at an all-time low, where I mostly felt lost in service to everyone else's needs and none of my own. It was two years where my business partner was learning, growing, stretching into all the things she was experiencing for the first time – how to run a business, think strategically, lead projects, manage staff, and think about cash flow. It was a huge learning curve for her, and I served as mentor, coach, and fellow do-er, helping to run the business, lead projects, and ensure business development happened.

As the days passed there was less and less time for creating anything new, rethinking my practice or building a new way of doing things in the public arena. I was needed to co-lead the business and deliver on projects. I needed to coach and mentor my new partner. I needed to set and guide direction and vision for the company.

We talked it through a few times, trying to come up with solutions to address the original idea of our roles and focus, but nothing really changed. I recalled a mentor of mine telling me decades ago that if you wanted to build a successful business you had to be all-in, and you needed to give up your day job. He always said that the risk and commitment would drive you to bring your ideas to life. I felt like my day job was the company with my new partner, and my dreams and vision of a new way of working in the public arena were my part-time business, done on weekends and evenings when I was too tired from fulfilling other responsibilities that I couldn't think or create, couldn't bring anything new to life.

Over time I got more frustrated, despondent, and hopeless. I woke up each morning a little more down, full of despair and resentment.

I imagine it's like staying in a marriage and going to counseling when you've already hired a divorce lawyer. I had come so far down the road of knowing I needed to leave the business and to reinvent my work, that taking on a business partner was a step that wasn't true to me, or to her. In my heart, I'd already left.

Finally, I went to my husband in tears and desperation and told him I needed to walk away. That the decision to keep the company going and take a partner had been one of the worst decisions of my life. I'd become someone who hated her job, who resented the company, was frustrated with her partner, and resented the work. I had no energy or creativity, and I was exhausted by the act of mentoring and coaching someone else to do the job I had wanted to quit. I had become someone I didn't like very much, and all I could think about was escaping.

Then I told my partner I was taking a leave of absence for a year, and the company was all hers.

Making Hard Decisions Opens New Doors

I wish I could say the transition was super smooth and easy, but it had bumpy, rocky moments like the ending of any relationship. It is a testament to her grace and commitment to our relationship that over a few months we were able to navigate our way through my departure from the company. We talked through what was needed, did the paperwork, and severed our partnership.

I was free! Free to start all over again, figuring out what I wanted to do with my career, what it looked like to work in conflict and high emotion in the public arena in totally different ways, and to build something brand-new.

It was terrifying and thrilling, exhausting, and energizing, and took everything I had ever known while stretching and growing me in countless new ways. It was full of failures, and small successes, and allowed me to rethink all the ways I had worked before, bringing me to this place, where this book and a new practice was born. It's the weaving of courageous leadership with brave, honest conversations that change our lives, organizations, and communities. It was joyful, reinventing decades of experience and yearning into new ways of working and living. It hasn't been easy, but it's been the right decision for me and every day I'm grateful for making the choice.

What Do You Really Want? What are You Yearning For? What are You Building?

They sometimes call them midlife crises, but I think they are really your soul waking up to demand what it really needs. The awakening is often born out of crisis – a divorce, loss of job, illness, or in my case, a public shaming. We often fight the yearning because it means our lives will become fundamentally different and change is always scary and difficult, even when it is positive. In leadership terms, they are often called the origin story – the moments of your life that drive you to make change real, and to establish a vision of something new that you are yearning for.

When I look back, I see that every brave, honest conversation must begin with yourself. These conversations are ongoing and iterative for me, but I'm seeing patterns that apply to the leadership of brave, honest conversations.

- **Stop hiding and allow yourself to see and feel the pain and yearning.**
  What are you hiding from? What are you ignoring, avoiding, or denying? What voice is becoming louder and louder so that you can't deny it any longer? What price are you paying when you shut down that voice? In order to begin this journey of leadership you have to stop running, and slowly turn to the mirror and be really, deeply honest with yourself. Only then in the stillness and clarity of your own pain, yearning, and hope can you see what really might be possible.

- **Listen to your heart and choose alignment with your authentic self.**
  When the truth of who you are and what you stand for is stripped bare, how might you live your life so that you honour yourself? The

story of my public shaming stripped me bare of what I thought I knew, believed in, and stood for. It also allowed me to begin again, redefining those things for myself as I slowly put myself back together. Only when you live from an authentic place, in service to the yearning and purpose that are calling you, can you make a positive difference in the world. When we try to be someone else, someone we think others expect us to be, we become a shallow copy of ourselves. It's easy when who you are and what you want matches what others want, but it takes enormous courage to step outside the confines of that box and choose something different. This isn't about putting yourself ahead of everyone else. It is about honouring yourself so you can be in service to others, making a difference, fulfilling the awakening of your soul to fulfill purpose.

- **Brave honest conversations with yourself are a precursor to brave, honest conversations with anyone else.**
  Having really difficult conversations with yourself, acknowledging and owning your own values, needs, commitments, and hopes is the foundation to being in conversation with others. When we have conversations from that place, we make decisions that are in alignment and that ease conflict and preserve relationships. If we don't do that, we find ourselves resentful, frustrated, despondent, overwhelmed, and stagnant. We aren't serving ourselves, and we aren't serving anyone else either. In my story, I harmed myself, and I harmed my partner too by not being able to fully own my needs, something I regret to this day.

- **You are all these things and so much more.**
  I've got a pretty tight relationship with the part of me that likes the word "should" and the part of me that likes the words "either/or." I'm learning again and again that those words almost always result in something with unintended consequences.

  'Should' can be a signal that I'm internalizing other people's expectations and need to check that those expectations are in alignment with my own values, hopes, needs and commitments. 'Should' can also be a signal that I'm making choices out of guilt and resentment.

'Either/or' thinking is a good opportunity for me to step back and consider what the situation might look like if I held a perspective of 'both/and'. I'm not responsible OR selfish; instead, I can be responsible to the needs of others AND honour my own values and needs by setting clear boundaries. I'm not only frustrated and ready for change; I'm frustrated, ready for change, and generous and compassionate to the needs of others.

When we hold that we are all these things, we extend our range and act from an integrated place. We are more capable and possible, and more likely to have a positive impact.

- **Know what you stand for, what you are committed to and come home to yourself.**
  Brave, honest conversations with yourself allows you to define your own values, needs, commitments, and hopes. This clarity serves as a touchstone to ground your decision-making, operating from an authentic place. When you've come home to yourself, you make choices and interact with others from a place of alignment. Everything becomes true, grounded, and centered. Your conversations with others have clarity, compassion, and curiosity.

These experiences are part of the journey that got me here. Failure, public shaming, choosing to live authentically with my strengths and shadows, getting clear on what I'm committed to, learning how to set boundaries, and knowing what I stand for, and want to build in the world. These are things that have contributed to my rethinking of how we interact, and the impact we have on each other when we are willing and able to have brave, honest conversations with ourselves and with each other.

Reflect and Practice – Exploring Your Leadership Commitment

A leadership commitment is something that outlines a bigger goal for leadership and helps you stretch and focus your development. It is grounded in your strengths and built on what you are yearning for and what you want to create in the world. The seeds of it are often found in your most memorable experiences.

To develop your own leadership commitment, consider your answers to these questions:

- What change do you want to create in the world?
- What unique strengths do you bring that will serve you to create this?
- What do you imagine and yearn for in the world?
- What do you want for yourself and also for others?

Articulate your leadership commitment in a sentence and come back to it regularly to see how it evolves. It will ground you and remind you of why you are doing the hard work of brave, honest conversations in the public arena.

Here is my leadership commitment:

I contribute to a world where leaders lead with courage, integrity, and compassion, having brave, honest conversations to solve the problems in our lives, organizations, and communities – together.

Reflect and Practice Recovering From Reactivity

Having a clear leadership commitment is crucial – and so is recovering when you are in a reactive state so you can make clear, thoughtful decisions.

Here are some practices to help you have brave, honest conversations with yourself and lead life's challenging moments with clarity and commitment.

Recovering from challenges or a reactive state

Leadership provides a never-ending opportunity to grow, learn, and to practice recovery back to self. This practice requires effort, mindfulness, and dedicated time. If you don't actively practice recovery, and raising your self-awareness, then you won't be as good at recovery as you would like.

This isn't about getting it perfect; instead, it is about learning and self-knowledge.

There is no simple solution to recovery. However, here are some tips to support you on this learning journey.

Practice mindfulness. Whatever that is for you, create a regular practice that results in space in your head and in your heart. Running, hiking, gardening, painting, writing, meditation – whatever it is, dedicating ongoing time to opening your mind and heart will allow you to have space in your reactions.

Recognize that the easiest path to recovery allows for a mix of being and doing. You will want to be willing to feel your reaction and emotions, create a pause before you respond, and then consciously choose what you will do.

It's a 3-step process
1) Acknowledge and own your reaction.
2) Pause and ask yourself what wisdom is there for you in this moment? Or ask yourself how you want to be in this interaction?
3) Respond.

If you have a difficult situation coming up, try these two things.

- Find a trusted friend, colleague or family member and **role play the situation, practicing your reaction.** This programs your brain into knowing responses that demonstrate what you want to experience, and responses that don't work.
- **Carve out some time to visualize and imagine the way you want a specific scenario to play out.** Imagine yourself leading with patience, compassion, and accountability. Imagining a future state generates the positive chemicals in your brain as if you had already had the positive experience. Bringing to mind this visualized state during the actual interaction will recreate that brain state and allow

you to recover to something your brain recalls, but you haven't actually experienced.

Part 1 grounds us in the messy business of being fully human, where failure is common and fear, self-doubt and shame may rise. When we can recover and learn from failure and embrace the whole of who we are, we can lead authentically. When we know what we are committed to, make choices in alignment with our values, and contribute to building something positive, we can begin the work of leading others. This is the path of leadership, and leadership begins with you.

PART 2

Shi(f)T Happens

Leadership in the Messy Middle With Others

In Part 2, we explore a world where people and groups collide headlong… and yet magic and possibility still happen. There are foundations of gathering we need in place for it to be possible for us to talk about hard things together. We find these basic practices in a combination of the things we do, and the ways we show up with each other, and leaders who make a positive difference have these skills, knowledge, and ways of being in their toolbox to draw on when a brave, honest conversation is called for.

CHAPTER 4

When You Think You Can Do Anything…

At this moment, I'm young, in the early stages of my career of shepherding large public conversations through the storm of emotion. With the naivety of youth, I'm certain I've got the answers to pull things off that others haven't yet managed. I've designed this conversation, for an impossible situation, and I'm pretty sure it's going to go well.

In my mind I'm thinking, *What could go wrong?* as if all my attention to details like fact sheets and microphone stands will invite community members to be thoughtful, peaceful, and kind about the proposed changes to their lives.

I'm standing on the stage of an auditorium, every seat filled with hundreds of angry, upset community members, a waiting line out the door of people wanting to come in but for whom there is no space. Moments ago, I called the fire department so they could manage the numbers of people who are admitted to the building.

On the stage behind me is a long table full of very important people: the area city councillors, the chief finance officer (CFO) for the local government and department heads for city planning, social services, recreation, and public works. The 'very important people' are all seated looking out into the crowd, each with a microphone and a pile of papers on the table in front of them.

The councillor gives me the nod, and despite the rumblings in the crowd and the people who can't get in the room, I take a breath and begin.

What You Don't Know Can Cause Harm

Looking back on this day, I have no recollection of being nervous, instead I'm full of excitement, certain that my approach to the conversation and the questions I have to ask these people will work out. I don't even realize I need courage for this moment. I'm mostly full of anticipation at how fun I believe this will be when people get into conversation. Years later, I set scenarios like this when I deliver training on how to lead brave, honest conversations and I forecast the inevitable train wreck that will roll down the track. At this moment, I'm too inexperienced to know what will come.

I welcome the crowd and thank them for coming and begin to explain how the evening will go. There are some jeers and shouts from the crowd, calling out, *"Shut up and sit down,"* and *"We came here to talk, not you,"* but I plow on. I introduce the 'very important people' on the stage, and then ask the CFO to begin his presentation on the city budget – a budget that outlines dramatic and drastic service cuts to all city services in order to reduce property taxes by 3 percent across the board. Ice rinks, pools, and libraries will have significantly reduced hours and many facilities will close. Grass cutting and pothole filling will be reduced, and people will have to pay for each bag of garbage they put out at the curb. Police officers, firefighters, and paramedics will be cut. There will be no more funding for affordable housing, and many social supports such as drop-in programs or wellness and health prevention programs will disappear. Transit fares will rise dramatically and the registration fees for recreation programs will almost double.

As the CFO continues his twenty-minute presentation, the crowd gets more and more agitated. Many are talking loudly to those beside them in the auditorium, the faces and body language of some are projecting a deep simmering rage, and there are shouts from the foyer as people who can't get into the auditorium hear snippets of the presentation. I can see that the foyer mob is getting angry and unruly.

City administration has been of the view that service reductions will be acceptable because everyone loves a tax cut, but they haven't taken the pulse of the quality-of-life city services bring to people's lives. Nor have they considered the inequitable impacts of service cuts, and who will bear the brunt of cost increases and lack of support. Looking back now with the wisdom of the years that have passed, I realize that many of the proposals for service reductions were probably intended to be political, to manipulate community members into recognizing the worth of city services and to make a tax increase more palatable.

Any time you take things away from people, changing what they know to something unfamiliar, they will react emotionally – it's just human nature. In today's climate, there are added implications when you further marginalize and overburden already fragile populations with public policy changes. I've been insulated from anticipating this possibility as a city employee, never questioning that the budget that is being presented is the real one the city will implement.

The CFO finishes presenting, and I ask if there are any questions. I've allowed five minutes in my agenda for questions of clarification on what was presented, and I invite people who want to clarify the budget numbers to come to the microphone stands. I repeatedly emphasize the words *'questions of clarification,'* letting people know that once we have the questions out of the way we will go into conversation groups.

An Eruption of Pent-up Emotion

What I don't anticipate is that the lineups at the two microphone stands set up in the aisles of the auditorium are now twenty or more people in each line and growing. I begin to take questions, frantically thinking about my agenda and timeline and a plan B of how to manage the situation.

The first questioner hasn't got a question – he's got a long litany of shouting comments and name calling about *"the buffoons on the stage who are being paid taxpayer money to ruin his life."* I ask the 'very important people' if they are willing to continue taking 'questions' and they nod their affirmation, because what else could they say in this moment? Every time a community member accuses the 'important people' of mismanaging the city, the crowd erupts in shouts and cheers, calling for staff to be fired.

One of my staff calls the police as a fight breaks out in the foyer, and the crowd in the auditorium seats is now standing and yelling every time a new person begins speaking at the microphone. I know the police are conferring about how to get the 'important people' out of the building if more violence erupts. We are forty-five minutes into a three-hour session and as my grandmother would say, everything has gone to *"hell in a handbasket."* I've got a microphone, and I'm trying to direct traffic, but no one can hear me over the shouting crowd.

Finally, out of desperation, I do the unthinkable – I signal to the audio person to turn off the microphones in the aisles. I pull out a chair on the stage and climb up on it. Now my mic is the only one working and I begin to talk loudly; *"Hold on, hold on. Can I have your attention? Can I get everyone's attention, please?"* It takes a few minutes, and then the crowd turns its gaze my way. An elderly man shouts, *"Listen here, missy, we don't want to hear from you!"* I respond with the naivety of youth, *"This isn't how I thought this evening would go! This whole thing is a disaster!"* Out of nervousness I laugh out loud. Some in the crowd and some on the stage chuckle with me; someone yells, *"You got that right, honey!"*

Finding a Plan B

I don't know what to do, so I tell them that, saying, *"This is not working, so would it be OK if we take a five-minute break and I figure out something different for tonight? I'm sure I can't come up with something worse than this!"* I see a few heads nodding and begin to take that for assent, but a man in the crowd yells, *"We don't care what you think. Get off the stage!"* and his assertion is countered by the elderly man who called me 'missy' a few moments earlier shouting back, *"Give the girl a break, Frank,"* he yells, and I've won five minutes to come up with a plan B.

I turn to the people on the stage and look at them. I am embarrassed and humiliated, and I'm also actively trying to problem-solve. I can lick my wounds later – right now I need to try to salvage something of this night. I propose that we give the crowd options – those who want to stay in the auditorium and ask 'questions' can line up at the microphone stands, and those that want to get into a conversation about the draft budget and talk about good idea / bad idea / changes needed can go to a number of smaller rooms for discussion where my staff will facilitate the discussion and take notes.

My original plan had been to move people to these breakout discussions based on the area of the budget the community most wanted to talk about, but clearly that kind of nuanced process is not going to work. Folks on the stage agree to stay and respond to questions, and my staff run off to the smaller rooms to get set up.

Within five minutes I turn back to the crowd and give them the options; *"If you want to stay and ask questions, these folks will stay and answer until you have no more questions. If you want to get into a conversation with your neighbours about the draft budget and talk about what is a good idea / bad idea / change is needed, go to one of the smaller meeting rooms out in the hallway there."*

I repeat it a couple of times and slowly people start moving. At least half the crowd filters out of the auditorium to the meeting rooms, which allows the people in the foyer to enter the auditorium. Over the next twenty minutes, the crowd in the auditorium thins to about twenty-five people.

Not everyone joins the meeting rooms; some take the time to tell me personally what a joke the draft budget and this consultation has been.

Some community members storm out and leave, angrier than when they came.

I move between meeting rooms, listening to the discussion, supporting my team, listening to the angriest people one on one. In the end, we go until everyone is talked out, hours past the time we were due to end the meeting.

Before we close up the building, we regroup –we've got another session planned for the next evening and we're going to need a different plan. For now, I'm going to go home and reflect on the disaster that unfolded.

There Are Always Lessons to Be Found

This was one of my first experiences with community rage in the public arena. So much of that anger and distrust is justified. The manipulation of community and the outright disrespect with which the city presented this draft budget, attempting to divide and conquer public sentiment, looking to create unrest at the prospect of losing city services so that people would support a tax increase, is so lacking in integrity that the folks on the stage (and those manipulating the political agenda from behind the scenes) should have been fired.

When we look at the total lack of trust in politicians and government, it stems from situations like this. Situations where the public can only react with a desperate outcry and then go through a sham consultation process, shouting to be heard.

My naivete of believing in the good intentions of professionals to do good work and set it out in good faith for public input was challenged from this experience. It turns out there are many organizations looking to manipulate and coerce a public response to generate an outcome that benefits their own agenda. These processes, done over and over again in democracies around the globe, damage public trust and increase public anger.

It's heartbreaking that in the name of democracy we put community members through these gruelling ordeals where they need to shout, yell, and literally fight their way to make their voices heard, and even then, they have no faith in the belief that their voices will impact the result.

This is not what democracy was meant to be. Democracy was designed for community members to come together and deliberate on important issues, coming to a better conclusion because they weighed each other's needs and perspectives, and then putting it to decision-makers who would represent community voice. Not everyone would get what they wanted, but in the end, all would be heard, and decisions would be made in good faith. That's not what happened at this meeting.

Shouting into a microphone stand, creating physical spaces that are adversarial and that divide people into who is important, and by inference, who is not important, not allowing people to talk about what matters most to them and instead focusing only on the technical details as if the needs, hopes, and lived experience of the humans who are being impacted by the technical details are not important. In this, we fail each other, and we further divide and separate people from the heart of what it is to be human in community with others. We lose that thread that connects us, and instead separate into camps, aligning with those who think the same as we do, and the polarization increases.

We need different ways of being with each other to talk about what matters, and a different kind of leader who is brave and kind enough to create the spaces that connect people to each other, despite the topic.

Reflect and Practice – Planning for a Meaningful, Constructive Conversation

What are you working towards when you bring people together into conversation?

The heart of democracy is grounded in the ability of people who care to gather and deliberate together on issues that matter and find a way forward together. Democracy exists not only in the public arena between government and citizens, but within organizations, communities, and in the depths of the human heart. We need to consider:

- How do we show up for each other?
- What are we focused on when we gather together?
- How honest, open, and thoughtful can we be when we interact with others?
- How transparent are we being with the information we are sharing and using to make decisions?
- How much integrity are we bringing to our discussion?
- How do we want people to feel when the conversation is over?
- What are our goals? What do we want to achieve or walk out of the conversation with?

- What do we want people to feel, understand, and experience when we are in conversation with them?

These are the questions to ask yourself *before* you begin; the questions everyone involved should be able to answer before we initiate difficult conversations. When we focus instead on only our own goals or agenda, the conversation becomes transactional, laden with details rather than values.

When we bring people together to talk about important things that impact their lives, we need to create space to welcome in their lived experience, values, needs, hopes, and concerns. We need to start the process talking about what they need in this conversation so they can show up fully and wholly and participate at their best.

We need to remember that the experts in the room are not only the folks with hierarchy and position, but also the folks with lived experience, experts in their own lives.

We need to be aware of the unjust and inequitable status quo, and take clear actions to reduce barriers to participation, so voices, needs, and perspectives can be amplified.

These are the spaces we want to create when we bring people together:

- Space for understanding and sharing before we go straight to problem solving.
- Small groups where people can share their experiences and hopes and connect with each other.
- Inclusive space where everyone can be in the conversation so loud and also quiet voices are heard.
- Sharing of needs, experiences, values, and stories, and fewer items on your agenda so there is time to talk about what is most important.
- Time to dive into passion, fear, worry, and emotion so our experiences are fully understood before you ask for comment, input, and feedback.
- Actively reducing barriers so that all voices are sought out and heard.

- Setups where the VIPs sit at the same level as their audience so everyone is held as equal, and all voices are valued.
- Circles, where voices, airtime and perspectives are equitable. Where feelings are embraced as a path to make meaning, and deepen understanding.
- Focus on respect, compassion, and transparency in initiating the tough discussion, and asking yourself how you would want to be treated if you were just learning about impacts on your life.

These are the basic building blocks of conversations that matter.

Reflect and Practice – Set Some New Norms for Tough Conversations in the Public Arena

Even the closest relationships struggle when pressure, emotion, or tensions are high. Having a set of shared agreements about HOW we interact with each other can guide us when things get difficult. Sometimes people call these ground rules, but I'd prefer to call them a conversation checklist, or shared agreements.

Ground rules imply you have the rules and will enforce the behaviours, attitudes, and actions of others. That often backfires. Whatever we call them, we are going to need to create something everyone can support, so we can move through challenging conversations together, and our discussions have a structure that supports connection and meaning.

What we experience when we talk together about important things lays the groundwork for connection, trust, relationships, and deeper understanding. When you have brave, honest conversations that create those four things, you can solve any problem.

As a best practice, you should create this checklist together with people before you begin discussion. Ask people to brainstorm:

- What do you need to participate at your best in this conversation? From yourself? From others?
- What might others need from you to participate at their best in this conversation? What could you contribute to the group?

Have people talk together in small groups and then share what they came up with. These ideas form the basis of the conversation checklist going forward, affirming that HOW we talk to each other is as important as WHAT we talk about.

Noted here, is my conversation checklist for brave, honest conversations.

CONVERSATION CHECKLIST

FOR BRAVE, HONEST CONVERSATIONS

○ When we are in this conversation, we are committed to being here for each other, no matter how messy it gets.

○ I will bring an open heart and curiosity, and I hope you will too.

○ We don't have to agree. We are committed to understanding each other's views, perspectives and experiences as deeply as possible.

○ I will share how this conversation makes me feel, even when I'm not sure why I'm feeling that way.

○ I will bring my courage and compassion, and I thank you for bringing yours.

○ I will hold a mindset of commitment and believe we can talk about tough stuff together. Will you?

○ We probably won't get things perfect or even exactly right. Let's care for each other rather than blame or shame each other.

○ We will take breaks and pause. We can come back to the conversation if we need to.

○ We will remind each other why we are having this conversation – to strengthen our relationship, to find solutions to tough problems together, and to understand each other and the issue better.

What else do we need?

_____

_____

_____

_____

CHAPTER 5

Best-Laid Plans Often Backfire

"They are not paying me enough money for this," I mumble to myself as I look around the room at the hundreds of people talking loudly to each other while big yellow school buses pull up outside the building.

I'm in a hot, stuffy, echoing, cavernous meeting room in Atlanta. I was hired to lead a workshop to find solutions to difficult challenges a community has been experiencing for years. I've led a few of these workshops before, convened by the Environmental Protection Agency (EPA), with representatives from the US Departments of Health, Housing, and Justice to hear from people directly about their needs.

This is a community at the forefront of environmental justice impacts; a contaminated site in the midst of their neighbourhood has resulted in the school closing, and there are people who are ill throughout the community. Poverty is exceptionally high, there is no nearby access to healthy food, and the associated effects of systemic racism are impacting generations.

Close to two hundred community members have gathered in this room for a conversation in a series of discussions with the EPA, which is making plans to address issues in this community and has convened its federal partners so they can take each accountability for problems within their scope. As with all things bureaucratic, the planning for this meeting has taken close to a year. Finally, now we are gathered together, and my role is to shepherd people's passionate, divergent perspectives and make sure community voices are heard.

As we prepare to begin, the EPA administrator rushes up to me with an urgent, frantic expression on her face, pointing toward the windows where the two school buses can be seen pulling into the parking lot.

"You need to go out there and tell those people they cannot come in. You need to tell them they are not welcome here."

I'm perplexed – who is on those buses and why can't they come in? And why am I telling them that? I ask her to clarify. *"It's the Tea Party. They've come to ruin the meeting. Go! Quick, before they get off the bus!"*

I'm pretty certain that my face reflects my incredulity.

I say, *"I'm not going to tell them they can't come in. This is a public meeting, and that will be the first media story tomorrow. But I will go talk to them."*

This meeting is being held as the Tea Party emerges as a populist force in US politics with an agenda to disband the EPA along with countless other platforms. The Party had been sending bus loads of supporters to interfere with EPA meetings across the country, regardless of their topic. Typically, they enter rooms with protest signs, placards, and chants, shutting down any possible constructive conversation and shouting at anyone who attempts to curtail their right to free speech.

Walking into the Fire

I find myself making my way towards the buses with no idea how I'm going to approach this situation, mumbling to myself, and rethinking my career choice. I have a room full of hundreds of community members eager to be heard, deserving of a voice and the possibility of having devastating challenges addressed, and a bus full of people who want to shut down that conversation.

The people in the room are mostly people of colour, and the people on the bus are primarily middle class, middle aged, white men.

I'm well aware of the perpetuation of the dynamics of oppression in this situation, and I don't have the first idea what to do. It's an impossible challenge I find myself in, with no good choices.

I can cancel the meeting, and send everyone home, and then no one gets their voice heard and the possibility of change vanishes.

I can tell the bus passengers they can't come in, but I have no way to enforce that, and since it's a public meeting the police won't bar their entry unless violence erupts.

I don't want to wait for violence to happen, so whatever I choose, that's top of mind for me. This community doesn't need any more challenges to deal with, and everyone deserves to feel safe.

As I stand in the sunshine in front of the first bus, a man steps off and walks towards me. He looks like he could be my grandfather; carefully trimmed white hair, blue eyes, and a jaunty plaid shirt. He is carrying a protest sign on a big stick that says, '*End the EPA*'. I take a deep breath, and smile at him.

I picture my Texan grandfather and channel my love for him.

"*Hi there,*" I say. "*What brings you here today?*"

We have a lengthy exchange where Ted (let's call him that, not his real name) asserts his right to break up the meeting, and I ask him questions to understand his hopes and plans. Most of the other folks stay on the bus, but the windows are open so they can listen to our conversation.

In the end, I say, "*Listen, Ted, here's the deal. This is a public meeting, so you've got a right to come in and I respect that right. Everyone has a right to participate in democracy. That means I respect the right of the folks back in the room waiting for me to get this meeting started too. If I think there is more shouting than listening going on, I will shut down the meeting because those rights aren't being respected. Can you agree to come in, and listen as much as you talk?*"

Ted mulls this over for a bit, confers with a colleague on the other bus, and agrees.

Then I say, "*I've got one more thing, Ted. You can bring your signs and posters in, and your buttons and petitions too. However, you're going to have to leave the sticks at the door. Can we agree to that too?*"

I'm referring to the long wood stakes the protest signs are attached to. I know from experience that if everything goes sideways in the session, these stakes are potential weapons. I tell Ted that my request is as much for his safety as the safety of the folks in the room. Ted finally agrees.

"*Then let's go. Let's get this meeting started,*" I say as I head back into the session.

I wish I could tell you it was this magical workshop, where people really dug in and embraced each other's perspectives, where harmony reigned, and everyone sat in a circle and hugged each other at the end.

It wasn't like that.

Make the Best Choice Available to You at the Time and Take Responsibility for Your Impact

It was wild, raucous, loud, and chaotic. It had moments of antagonism, high emotion, and a few shouted interactions.

There were also beautiful moments where people who had never previously been in conversation learned from each other, where some Tea Party folks began to understand why the meeting mattered to this community, and what positive change it could bring.

I had to stand on a chair a couple of times, waving my arms and calling into a microphone to get people to pay attention when the emotional temperature rose too high. While we managed to document the changes needed by the community so they could be addressed by the federal departments present, we were often sidetracked by the dynamics and group interaction, so the discussion wasn't as deep and rich as it could have been.

I once told this story in a training session and a participant called out and questioned my choice to allow the Tea Party folks into the room. She highlighted that doing so perpetuated systemic racism and didn't really allow the community to be fully heard. It took something away from those already marginalized to give something to those who already hold power. I think she was right. And also, I'm not sure that at the moment I would have made a different choice.

There is no map or guidebook for difficult choices. There is only your own internal barometer that tells you if you are honouring your values, acting in integrity with them, and making choices you can stand behind. I hold deep values of fairness, equity, and a right to a voice. In this situation, the value I managed to honour was a right to a voice.

Was it fair or equitable that those folks showed up in busloads and were admitted to the meeting? No.

Was it democracy? Yes.

Is democracy imperfect and the system influenced by years of systemic racism and inequities? You bet.

Is there another system open to us? Not right now.

We've got to reimagine and recreate the system we have through small moments and interactions, doing the best we can with what we've got while we advocate, protest, call for, and work to change the system for the better.

Reflect and Practice – How Do You Choose to Lead in Difficult Situations?

Life is full of impossible situations where there are no good choices.

Sometimes all you can do is ask yourself some difficult questions:

- What are you committed to?
- What do you stand for?
- What is this moment calling for from you?
- What can you choose that you can take responsibility for?

These questions require a practice of slowing things down for yourself, awareness versus reaction, reflection versus immediate action. Sometimes you might have to reflect and consider quickly. But no matter your time frame, ideally you want to be able to walk away at the end and be sure you are standing in your own values, clear on your intentions and impact.

Reflect and Practice – What 'Side' Are You On?

It is human nature to seek to align people with us, to connect around a common belief, and when that happens to become certain in the rightness of our view. We then tell ourselves a story about our side that affirms how right we are – and how wrong anyone else is.

It is natural to choose a story or perspective and feel convinced in the rightness of that perspective or position. In a similar way to when we lead from the story we are telling ourselves, we can choose a 'side' to stand in and lead from. However, when we do that, we often become more committed to our view, perspective, or story than to all the people who might be in the conversation, or who we might find common ground with. We become more committed to our perspective than we do to moving forward WITH others. Working WITH others is an aspect of holding the whole, rather than holding one limiting story or perspective, and is a core leadership competency.

To lead brave, honest conversations we want to create a continual practice of building your awareness of your 'sides' (or stories) in your interactions so you can choose to lead in ways that bring people with you, rather than polarizing into extreme sides. When your awareness increases, your conscious choice-making increases and you build the foundation for enrolling and empowering others.

It can be easy and natural to pick a side on an issue, and to choose certainty and the satisfaction of feeling like you are right (and others are wrong). It is so common to pick a side or perspective, especially when we feel strongly about something, and to find ourselves more committed to the side we are on than to the people we are in conversation or relationship with.

Instead, in a brave, honest conversation we want to move away from the sides of righteous certainty into the space between us and others. When we hold that space, we become more committed to relationships, connection, and trust than we are to being right. Consider these questions:

- What issues have you taken a side on and where have you ended up?
- Who was 'with you' and who was 'against you'? Did the sides get closer together or further apart?
- What impact do you have when you are committed to being right or leading from your side or story?
- How can you move from an either / or position to an AND position where you hold your own views and also hold curiosity for the views of others at the same time?

Reflect and Practice – Calling People in Versus Calling Them Out

There is a distinct difference in feeling, experience, and result, between calling something out and calling something in.

When we call something out, we forcefully declare a behaviour, words, or action to be wrong. We take a stand and say to the world that this is not OK with us. In the case of explicit and overt hate, hurt, violence, and discrimination we need to take a stand. We need to declare the kind of world we value and are building and stand firmly in what we believe in; advocating for what we want.

However, sometimes when we call something out, we righteously make more than the actions, words, or behaviours wrong, and we make the person wrong. We can slide into blame, shame, and condemnation in ways that inflame and amplify the conflict, and even dig people into their position. We can slide into wanting to present ourselves as right as much as, or more than we want to make something (or someone) else wrong. Sometimes that might be the right thing, depending on the situation, and sometimes it isn't. Calling out is best done cleanly without blame, shame, or ego.

When we call people in, we identify the negative impact of their words, actions, or behaviours and we invite them into a conversation focused on learning, growth, information sharing, and understanding, that hopefully results in new ways of thinking and acting. We avoid blaming or shaming an individual, which leaves them open to the possibility of new perspectives and information, which can create positive change.

I was recently on vacation in French Polynesia and spent a day visiting the island of Huahine. I booked a guided tour to explore and learn about the sacred sites and history of the Polynesian people. With more than a thousand years of history in the islands, I was curious to begin to learn about the culture, values, practices, and worldviews of the people who live in this magical part of the world.

Our guide turned out to be a resident of Huahine, who had relocated there from the United States over twenty-five years ago, married a Polynesian woman, and was raising his family on the island. Let's call him George (not his real name). George was of European descent and had a background in anthropology and had even worked on the archaeological excavation of one of the ancient sites on the island.

At the start of the tour George extolled the benefits that colonisation by France had brought to Polynesia, giving examples of education, minimum wage, infrastructure, health care, and subsidized services like air lines and more. He noted that 80 percent of Polynesians want to retain the governance structure as part of France. After describing only the virtues of French colonisation, George proceeded to voice his opinion to our group that any harms that were done in the past were in the past, and were done by others, not by him. He suggested that everyone should focus on moving forward instead of looking back.

I have to admit that I negatively reacted to his views, and I reflected only on my experience with the impacts of colonialism in Canada when I responded to his opinions in front of the group. If I'm totally honest, my ego led my response. I asked, *"In Canada, there have been many conversations and initiatives related to reconciliation, and we are just beginning to unravel the complexities of our shared history. You've mentioned the benefits of colonisation by France, but you haven't mentioned any negative impacts – can you tell us about those? What is the state of reconciliation here?"*

Now these might sound like remarks by a reasonable person, but I know I was irritated and frustrated with his comments and wanted to assert myself as right, calling out that he could expand his thinking and to infer that he was wrong.

At first, he rejected my comments and question, saying that what had happened in the past had been the actions of those long gone, and those things weren't his deeds to unravel, acknowledge, or rectify. Many in the group agreed with him, and one person from the USA referenced the situation with Native Americans, affirming that what was done in the past was done, and moving forward is the only answer. I let it go, but I could tell that it was on George's mind, as it was on mine.

Later in the day, George made more comments: how Polynesians had an oral history, and nothing was documented…therefore there was no way to know what was true; that Polynesians had converted to

Christianity…therefore their ancient sites meant nothing to the present-day people. The language was no longer taught in schools…therefore, the language of the islands was French and then English, and the only place for people to learn their language was if their families continued to speak it.

Close to the end of the tour, George approached me and said, *"You've made me think. There might be another way to look at things."*

I responded and said, *"I wonder too, if I should consider that every situation of colonisation is different, and the experiences I am familiar with aren't transferable to other parts of the world. Just because I know something, doesn't mean it is true everywhere."*

Our conversation continued, with each of us loosening our hold on what we held to be certain, absolute, and true, to learn a little more about another experience or perspective. We didn't solve any problems or challenges, instead we met each other part way along, and saw things a little differently as a result.

Calling someone out communicates that they are wrong. Calling someone in communicates that the conversation could continue, and that there is something to learn and explore by all. It isn't always done with grace, and when emotion is present it can be awkward or laced with ego, but it can open a door, bridge a divide, and contribute to growth on all sides.

Tips to call someone out

When you need to call someone out, you can say things like:

- That comment was really offensive. Can you choose a different word or language?
- I need to push back on what you said. I disagree.
- I don't find that funny or amusing. I find it hurtful and/or offensive.
- I feel obligated to tell you that what you just said is not OK with me.
- Based on what you just said, I can't be in this conversation any longer.

Tips to call someone in

When you want to call someone in, you can say things like:

- I'm having a strong reaction to what you just said, and I'm trying to stay curious. What experiences led you to that view?

- My perspective is different than yours and I'm curious how you came to that conclusion? Can you tell me more about your experience?

- You may not realize this, but I have some experience with what you are talking about. I wonder if we could learn more about each other's experiences.

- I wonder how someone else different than us might see this situation?

- What is true for you in this situation?

- What makes you uncomfortable, worried, or anxious about this situation?

- How might your words or actions impact others?

- What is another way to look at this situation?

Calling someone in creates the opportunity for shared understanding, strengthened relationships, and shifts in perspective.

CHAPTER 6

Safe and Brave Spaces for Conversation

There are moments when seeds are planted, and growth happens. Sometimes you can only see it when you look back and identify the exact situations where things changed.

These are the moments that have changed the course of my practice, shaken me to my core, made me rethink and question how it is we talk together, connecting to our humanity so we can solve the problems we face.

These moments are mostly hard-won, usually full of failure, mistakes, and wrong steps. They are moments where I learned deeply because the options were quitting or growing. Sometimes they come from moments of joy or possibility, but mostly they come from difficulty and challenge. They planted seeds so that now when I line them up, they are ready for harvest.

When You Are Nervous You Know it Matters

I'm standing in a parking lot, taking deep breaths, doing my usual routine to steady my nerves before I lead a tough conversation. I'm distracted by swarms of biting black flies, swatting them away, walking in big circles, hoping I'm fast enough to outrun them, when a white pick-up truck races into the lot, spraying gravel as it pulls up beside me.

I'm here to lead a conversation with employees of the hydroelectric dam in this remote northern community, employees who live in the adjacent indigenous community where residents are threatening a blockade of the dam. I've been brought in to figure out if there is a way forward, heading the company and the community towards a better relationship, and to figure out what that looks like.

So, I'm in the parking lot, trying to take deep breaths between the swarms of black flies, secretly worried I'm not up to the task. The engine turns off in the truck and a man emerges in a ball of fury, energy pulsating as he heads my way. It's just the two of us out here in the parking lot, and the breaths I'm trying to take catch in my throat.

He comes right up to me, inches away, his face is flushed, sweaty, and screwed up in an expression of ferocious disdain. He points his finger in my face and yells, *"Who do you think you are? You white girl riding in on your white horse, thinking you are coming in here to save us? Do you think because your last name is McCallum you've got some free ride here? You are no different than all the rest of them. Coming in saying nice things, and then leaving and nothing is different. Nothing!"*

He's got spit at the corner of his mouth and now he's waiting for me to answer his questions.

I take a step back, even though I know I probably shouldn't. If this was a training course I was teaching, I'd tell students to take a deep breath to calm their nervous system and lean into the conversation with an open heart. But that's in training. Here in this moment one part of my brain is thinking, *"Holy shit, where is everyone else? Haven't they heard this from inside? What am I going to do?"* Instead, I say, *"I'm just here to listen, hoping to understand. What do you need me to know?"*

I feel deeply inadequate – what could I possibly say in response to what I see as his fully justified rage? He is right – I'm a white woman in service to finding a solution, probably in a long line of white people showing up saying they've got the answers to the problems their ancestors created.

My last name is McCallum; it's my husband's last name. When the residents of this community agreed to talk to us, my name spread like wildfire through the area. The chief of the local First Nation has the last name of McCallum. To my knowledge we aren't related, but I'm sure way back there is a connection. That's irrelevant to this moment, but my mind is darting in circles like a frightened bird trying to escape a cage.

My response seems to give him pause. He leans back on his heels, away from the balls of his feet, slightly away from me. *"I'm here because I was told I had to be here by my boss. This whole conversation is bullshit. I'm looking at you – if something doesn't change you better watch out."* He turns and storms away, heading towards the building, where people are gathered for me to lead them in conversation.

Well, that's a great fucking start, I think. I swat away a couple more black flies and follow him into the building. Here goes nothing.

What Does it Mean to Feel Safe in a Conversation?

Everyone says they want the space of a conversation to be safe, but I think what they really mean is they want other people to be nice and respectful. I think people say that they want a safe space when they want everyone to think like they do, with harmony and sweetness flowing through our veins, everyone in total agreement.

Really, when the stakes and the impacts are so high, is that possible? I don't think we are going for nice and harmonious in those moments – or if we are, we are dreaming. I don't think 'nice' gets us to solutions. What if instead we went for honest, vulnerable, willing to tell the real story and talk about the real impacts? What if instead of looking for the 'safe space' we looked for the space where we really see and hear each other?

What if we Looked for the Brave Space Instead of the Safe Space?

What if we cut each other some slack when things really matter?

What if we recognize that the stuff that matters the most makes us really, really passionate, and has us feel really deeply?

What if instead of judging people's reactions as right or wrong we leaned into the moments of brutal honesty so we could learn more?

What if we just bear witness to each other's pain and heartache?

Isn't it true that some people will never feel "safe"?

Isn't it true that because of impacts of colonisation, systemic discrimination, violence or trauma, the conversation is never going to feel safe?

What if instead of safe we created space where we felt *safe enough* to be willing to tell our stories, to tell our truths? One of my truths is that I am that white woman in this indigenous community, and while I have skills, experience, and knowledge to work with conflict I'm not sure my ancestry makes me the right person to lead this conversation. I need to own that and also look at the impact it will have on the process.

Emotional and Physical Safety in Difficult Situations

To this point I've gone into countless situations where the stakes and emotions are high, and I've not thought a lot about my own physical safety. I've had this unfailing belief in the goodness of other people to naively think my faith will protect me.

We are all the products of our previous experiences and I'm the daughter of a cop, and I can hear him telling me that you never know what people can do when pushed to their edges. I think it's time I start thinking about the physical and mental health of participants, my team, and myself in these tough conversations.

I think we need to start creating safety plans for these difficult discussions, to keep all of us well enough for the next tough conversation. Let's create brave spaces where we do the hard work of talking about important things, and let's be honest that safe spaces may be unrealistic or unproductive to our goal of deeper understanding, of difference, of creating connection, and allowing relationships to grow.

Reflect and Practice – Creating a Brave Space

What makes a space safe?

What makes a space brave?

These are distinctly different questions.

A safe space brings to mind images of security, caring, and comfort. These are beautiful things to have in a conversation but are they common in conversations where vastly different values, perspectives, experiences, or needs are at play? It's possible but less likely.

Sometimes safety is used as a synonym for harmony, but brave, honest conversations require us to dig into differences and expand our understanding of each other in order to deepen connection. With that can come emotion and discomfort – but those things aren't bad.

Instead, we can think about emotion as a path to make meaning, and discomfort as a sign we are talking about the real and important things. A safe space full of harmony can actually be a barrier to creating true understanding and connection because we could be stifling dissent or divergence in the interests of sameness and calm.

Instead, what if we created a brave space for difficult conversations?

Whether you are planning a brave, honest conversation one-on-one or in a group, start the discussion with a conversation about brave space. Here are some comments and questions to get you started:

- We know this could be a passionate, emotional conversation where we talk about difficult issues. In order to do that, we will each need to be brave. What does it mean to you to be brave? Go around and share answers and offer some additional thoughts. Brave requires vulnerability and an open heart, being willing to share your feelings, thoughts, hopes and fears. Brave is being afraid and showing up anyway, committed to deeper understanding, relationship, or connection.
- What will you need from others in order to be brave in this discussion? Ask people for their ideas. Helpful suggestions can include: speaking for yourself with "I" statements, taking breaks and pauses, acknowledging when emotion is rising and taking a

moment to identify what is causing the rise, staying curious versus reactive, taking responsibility for the impact of our words and actions on others.

If we are going to move forward on difficult issues and increase understanding, then we will need to be willing to step into and stay in discomfort. Discomfort can be a place of creativity, innovation, and new ideas. It can be a place of wonder, curiosity, and possibility. Our choice of perspective impacts whether we see discomfort as something to run from or something to run towards. Our path through difficulty comes with discomfort but avoiding discomfort won't get us through the challenges.

Chapter 7

Leading Through Chaos and Disruption

I'm in a sprawling complex spread across beautiful gardens on the slopes of Mount Macedon in Australia. This place is the home of the Australian Emergency Management Institute and I've been brought here to work with a group of disaster response specialists, community support agencies, and community members affected by natural disasters like bushfires and cyclones. My job is to unpack and reflect on how to put community at the very centre of the disaster recovery cycle. I've been tasked with supporting the group as they focus their approach to community led recovery to disaster from a heart centred place, building capacity to embrace and work with the intense emotions, trauma, conflict, and impacts that result from living through the aftermath of a massive upheaval.

It's a beautiful spring morning, with light dew on the ground, and the scent of eucalyptus in the air as I make my way from my dorm room to the cavernous meeting space to prepare for the day and centre myself for the conversation. I enter the room and flip on the lights, scanning the room to see if the seventy-five chairs are set in a large open circle. In the very centre of the circle is the biggest spider I've ever seen, the size of my hand all spread out, sitting peacefully as if waiting for the conversation to commence.

I'm brave when it comes to a room full of angry, fearful, or grief-stricken people, but a lone giant spider pauses me in my tracks. I

73

choose the cowardly response and decide to pretend it isn't there while I go about preparing the room. Eventually, my Australian co-facilitator arrives and gently slides a piece of paper under it and pops a bucket over the top and drops it outside, as if nothing interesting has happened. Fear is a universal human response, but what triggers it for me will be different than what triggers it for you. It's an important reminder that context is everything, and what is familiar to each of us is different when our environment has shifted.

Participants gather; they stroll into the room in ones and twos, expecting to sit at desks or small tables beside colleagues for this workshop. They've got notebooks and pens, ready to take notes, expecting a lecture.

Everyone Wants the Easy, Linear, Smooth Path

Everyone is looking for the checklist and the worksheet, the easy-to-follow step-by-step guidance that tells you exactly how to work with high conflict and emotion within the community in deeply challenging situations. They have this hope, which I'm about to shatter, that this expert from Canada will share the magic ingredients for the recipe that gets you peace and harmony when things are tough.

I know I'm going to disappoint them because there is no magic recipe, and there definitely isn't a checklist, or a worksheet.

We gather in one large circle with no tables, and we sit, quietly, in silence. I begin talking softly, intentionally, with pauses between my words and sentences, inviting in a deeper listening, inviting in a gentle discomfort, settling people into being together.

I've learned that how you show up, and what you stand for matters most in these conversations. Not your knowledge, role, or position. Not your answers or the technical details. The energy and emotion I bring to this conversation impacts the space.

Can you be loving and kind when others are full of rage, anxiety, and rigidity?

Can you set boundaries with a generous heart when others are rolling with chaos and fear?

Can you invite people to find their feet in discomfort and fear and stay long enough to seek the meaning and the wisdom the experience presents?

That is the foundation of what it takes to lead brave, honest conversations in moments like this.

Unbeknownst to this group, we've chosen to lead this five-day session by opening the circle, settling them in, and connecting them to each other. Then we will be launching them into teams via a simulated disaster. This will play out their reactions and responses to putting people at the centre of the recovery cycle, inviting growth and learning. The session is fully immersive and experiential, grounded in doing and then reflecting. I give the opening circle about sixty minutes, settling people in, opening their hearts, transitioning to this way of being together and then I give a nod to my colleagues.

The Experience Lays the Foundation for Transformation

They run in the room shouting and crying that the mine has caved in, and the mountain of slag has collapsed, enveloping part of the town and the school. We've chosen to simulate the tragic Aberfan, Wales, coal mine disaster that happened in 1966 in the hopes that no one in the room will have personal experience with the situation.

I tell people the workshop has begun and to reach under their chairs to see instructions about which team they are on. I will see them back in this room in four hours for their first situational report. That's it for instructions – they are on their own now in the midst of chaos and disruption.

I like to think that a crisis is a horrible thing to waste; and a simulated crisis allows us to see our strengths and our shadows in a space where we can harvest the learning from our reactions, actions, and choices. Over the next five days, day and night, they will work to grow as leaders, creating space for connection, trust, and relationship in the face of impossible circumstances.

As a leader of challenging conversations, there are moments when the magic happens, when you can feel the shift in the room, when people harness the best of themselves and bring it to others, in service to the work and the conversation.

When I tell the group they have begun, there is the usual bewilderment, confusion, and discomfort…and then the surge of energy as they rise to the challenge, stepping into the chaos and confusion. There are always some who hang back, who want certainty, who are more attuned to their own fear and discomfort than what the moment calls for from them.

That is OK – this is hard, uncomfortable work, and everyone is at a different stage of their journey. There will always be a few who step aside, retreating to their phones or computers, even inventing family, or work emergencies so they can avoid the discomfort of not having a playbook or rules to follow. That is also OK – there is enormous learning, no matter how they show up or choose to respond. We will unpack and explore the dynamics, emotional response, and leadership choices they all made in these moments whenever we reconvene as a group.

We will especially consider if they moved right to task and action when they found their groups or if they took moments to settle in and focus the new team on being, mindset, and what they were committed to as a group. The teams that connect to each other, that focus on values, commitments, and roles, that remind themselves of the bigger picture of centering community, the teams that begin their journey with *being* rather than *doing,* will be more successful over the five-day journey.

Finding Our Own Courage and Compassion to Do Hard Things With Others

In Parker Palmer's beautiful book *Healing the Heart of Democracy,* Terry Tempest Williams talks about the human heart being the home of democracy. When we come home to ourselves and find our own compassion, courage, and integrity we can be in conversation with others to relentlessly engage with our neighbours and fellow citizens in the most important conversations.

This is the essence of the learning in this room in Australia – how do they put people at the very centre of the disaster recovery approach? What does it mean to walk into the fire of emotion, to stand with someone who is suffering, to call forth their needs and hopes to begin the rough and bumpy recovery process? How will they dance with urgent need for action, tasks, and getting things done with the slow, gentle pace of being of service to fellow human beings who are suffering? How will they embrace the emotion and work with it, seeing it as a path to making meaning and finding resolution? These are the lessons of the next five days.

Understanding Chaos and Disruption

The words chaos and disruption get thrown around a lot in these times. In leadership articles I see headlines like, 'Thriving in Disruption,' or "Innovating When Chaos Strikes," and I wonder if we have a shared understanding of what those words mean in the public arena. Chaos and disruption are perfect words to describe the impacts of natural disaster, war, polarized conflict, and events like a global pandemic.

When I use the word 'disruption' I mean a catastrophic and fundamental shift in what we can depend on or know for certain, where what we had planned or could solve isn't possible anymore. It's a confusing, uncertain, overwhelming place where complexity or chaos reigns.

When I use the word 'chaos' I think about what happens in our brain so that we slide into depression, pessimism, hopelessness, fear, guilt, and emotional overwhelm, ill-equipped to solve the very challenges we are facing. If that is what we personally feel and experience, I refer to the work of Dave Snowden, in his decision-making framework *The Cynefin Model*, where chaos is one of the unordered domains where standard linear problem solving doesn't work, and no one expert has the answers, but experience can be helpful. We need structure and safety at first, and then we need to let go of what we thought we knew and come at the situation from totally different angles. This is exactly what happens in natural disasters, and also in polarized conflict. Safety and structure first, then letting go of what we thought we knew, choosing different perspectives and creating an entirely new way forward.

Disruption and chaos are words that characterize our times. They are why we need a different kind of leadership to solve the challenges we face. Leaders can lead in chaos and disruption, but it requires different skills, knowledge, and ways of being than it takes to lead in regular or complicated situations.

In these times, we need equal parts doing (actions we take) and being (mindset, attitudes, and behaviours) to be effective.

Doing and Being Are the Building Blocks of Leadership in Chaos and Disruption

LEADERSHIP TRAITS

FOR CHAOS AND DISRUPTION

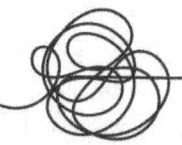

DOING - Leadership actions that serve us in chaos and disruption

BEING - Leadership mindset, attitudes and behaviours that serve us in chaos and disruption

Skills and knowledge to bring people together to brainstorm, share, contribute and problem-solve, drawing on the wisdom and experience of the collective

Commitment to a greater purpose outside of oneself and the skills to communicate a way forward that invites others in to be part of the solution, creating momentum

Ability to provide structure and safety in uncertain times and a place to gather in conversation with others

Trying, testing, failing and learning a way forward focused on progress over perfection

Making meaning and sense from patterns and events to apply the knowledge to new ways of working and living

Capacity to bring others along on the journey of change

Humility to acknowledge we don't have all the answers, and it will take more than us to lead all of us together out of the challenges

Courage to stand in the fire of uncertainty, anxiety, fear and grief and welcome in the fullness of human experience in chaos and disruption

Empathy for the challenges we experience, so that people do not feel alone in the wild and are supported on this journey

Creativity and a willingness to be wrong in service to finding a way forward by trying and failing in developing solutions

Sensing the patterns and markers of change in the system and letting go of the status quo with an open heart and open mind

Commitment to centering humanity and people in the challenges

Leading with authenticity, honesty and integrity

These are the skills, knowledge, and ways of being we reinforced that week in the spring sunshine at Mount Macedon. The dance of being and doing is core to leadership in chaos and disruption.

Reflect and Practice — Dancing with BEING and DOING

The human heart is the centre of everything – our beliefs, feelings, needs, and values guide and motivates every choice we make. When we centre others at the heart of our conversations and seek to really see them as they are, not as we want them to be, we begin the process of transformation.

We can often be tempted to centre the issue, opinions, challenges, and facts of the checklist to progress at the centre of our conversations. When we do that, we can often create barriers and distance between each other.

Instead, we must first connect to each other, then tackle the issues. If we tackle the issues without connecting to each other, our likelihood of success is far lower. When we are connected and, in a relationship, we can solve almost any challenge. This practice requires a mix of BEING and DOING.

- BEING is your mindset, perspective, behaviours, and how you show up, grounded in the array of unique strengths available to you.
- DOING are the actions, tasks, and activities we undertake to resolve or transform an issue.

For example, in a recent conversation with a client on a highly controversial public issue, I asked these questions focused on BEING:

- How do you want to be seen and perceived?
- What do you want people to feel or experience when you speak with them about this issue?
- What do you want them to remember about your interaction with them?

- How do you want to show up? What strengths can you lean into that will serve these people and this situation?

His answers to these questions included wanting to be seen as trustworthy and open, having people feel like they matter, and for them to be reassured he is taking action to protect them in this difficult time. He wanted them to know he is doing everything he can, but that he doesn't have all the answers...yet. He wanted to welcome the idea that perhaps they have answers that are better than his and he is inviting them to the table to find a way forward.

He chose to show up with honesty, courage, candor, and compassion. This is the 'being' that will serve him in this challenging situation.

When we think about DOING – the actions, tasks, and activities that will address a situation, the questions I ask include:

- What actions or activities will move this issue forward or address concerns?
- In what ways can you be responsive to the challenges you are facing?
- What actions will create a sense of movement?
- What information will people need so they understand the situation? What other information will be needed to allow for deeper understanding?

We need to consider both the being and doing that will serve the people and the situation we find ourselves in order to move forward.

If we rely too heavily on being we can create positive feelings and perceptions, but there will be a lack of momentum or action, and this can result in stagnation and lack of trust.

If we rely too heavily on doing things, we will get things done and make progress, often at the expense of relationships and create a perception that we don't care about others. It is a dance that requires steps in both directions.

When you face a leadership challenge fraught with chaos and disruption take a few moments and work through the questions for yourself. Your results will be improved and your approach more effective as you dance with being and doing.

Reflect and Practice — What Position Are You Leading From?

It requires consciousness and intentionality grounded in self-awareness to lead challenging conversations in chaos and disruption. There are multiple positions of leadership you can take when you participate in a difficult conversation. These include:

- Leading Self
- Leading From the Front
- Leading From the Side
- Leading From Behind
- Leading From the Space

Leading Self

This is where all leadership begins—from within. It begins with taking responsibility for who you are, knowing your values, and then leading in alignment with those values.

Self-awareness is about seeing who you are in relation to those you impact and asking yourself if this is the person you want to be. Opening your heart is not enough. The bigger question is what is motivating your heart so that your deep self-knowledge is grounded in a commitment to the situation and the people.

Leading self is grounded in self-acceptance, and powerful self-knowledge, creating the capacity to act with integrity in alignment with your values.

Leading From the Front

Leading in front is not necessarily about being in charge. Leading from the front requires a connection with the people who are following you and standing firmly for a clear direction and purpose. Leading from the front is where you hold the vision, and also inspire and engage others.

Leadership is not a solo enterprise, so you don't lead alone – you take others with you. You do not need to have all the answers but instead capture and leverage the talents of those around you, generating collaboration, providing direction, and blazing the way forward.

Leading From the Side

Two can be better than one. Leading from the side is about partnering with others. Harnessing people's collective genius, where there is a dance between leading and following and the blend allows for disagreement, spontaneity, and respective strengths to shine.

Leading from the side requires trust on both sides, leaning into another for support and help, willing to follow and then to lead, as the partnership moves forward.

Leading from the side requires a shared vision and intention and supporting each other's strengths to generate a powerful synergy in which the whole is much greater than the sum of the parts. Leading from the side is about blending, merging, and mutual trust in service to a shared goal, growth, or purpose.

Leading From Behind

This is about service. When you lead from behind you focus on providing whatever is needed, and through openhearted engagement that can look like support, encouragement, silence, and challenge.

Leading from behind is core to empowering and enabling others by encouraging, supporting growth, learning, and capability. Leaders who lead from behind act like coaches, focusing on being of service.

Leading From the Space

Leading from the space is about tapping into the energy of the emotion, community, organization, history, and situation, and expanding your attention beyond individual people to connect with intuition, instinct, and the system you are working in.

Leading from the space allows you to be open to the unknown, and to tap into what is happening around people or the issue, integrating things in a holistic view.

Ask yourself what else is here that hasn't been voiced? What needs to be known and what are you blind to in order to practice leading from space?

As you embark on your next challenging conversation, ask yourself what position of leadership will serve you in this situation, with these people, knowing that the traditional position of leading from the front is only one of many options?

CHAPTER 8

Just Enough Structure to Contain a Challenging Conversation

Much of my career is made up of moments of imposter anxiety where I look back and think to myself, *Who do you think you are?*

This is another one of those times where all I know is that I'm committed to this sweet, precious conversation, listening deeply to what is happening in this moment, certain that I'm making it up as I go because there isn't a guidebook for this stuff.

I've been hired to design a community engagement process, and build community capacity to implement that conversation, with a goal to improve health outcomes in seven First Nation communities across northern Ontario, Canada. It's a richly complex topic, layered with the impacts of colonisation, cultural values, and protocols, and ways of knowing and being that challenge a system of healthcare delivery that is clinical, linear, and focused on symptoms rather than prevention.

There is nothing simple or easy about the conversation, and nothing more important in public health than putting people at the centre of improving their own health outcomes, and the outcomes of their communities.

I'm in a community centre in a small First Nation community in northern Ontario filled with the scents of coffee, bannock, and jam, leaning in to listen to the wisdom of elders and community members about what will make this long-term conversation meaningful and effective. The room is steamy and smells of wool, as people come in from the cold and snow outside and settle into chairs in the overheated room.

I'm holding tensions; the organization that has hired me is a health research institute and they want metrics, indicators, milestones, and timelines for the engagement process and outcomes. In contrast, the community wants to unpeel the layers of wisdom, leaning into what isn't working for them, and what might be better, and how they want to be with each other as they embark on this journey.

I keep thinking back to that spider in the middle of the circle of the chairs in Australia – these tensions create a web of interconnections, relationship, conflict, and complexity we must work with in order to move forward. Like a spider's web, there is beauty and also places we can get trapped.

Worldviews are in conflict; I've tried explaining to the health institute that their approach and way of working likely isn't going to work here, and now I'm creating space for the community to share what they think will work best. After that, we will do the hard work of reconciling those views.

Structure as a Container for Challenging Conversations

In this workshop (one of many), we are talking about the engagement process and how to bring this conversation to the community so all voices are valued and heard. I also know we are deep in the experience of the conversation ourselves, settling into how it will feel for others as participants experience it for themselves.

I introduce a Socratic Circle – which is a talking circle in two layers.

There is an inner circle of people who have the voice, who carry the conversation, who have the opportunity – not the obligation – to speak.

There is an outer circle spread around the inner circle like a blanket or a hug, holding them in their conversation. The outer circle doesn't speak. People in this circle listen deeply to understand what is being said, and what is not being said, to hear the patterns and insights between the words, in the tone, body language, and energy of the inner circle.

At some point a bell is rung and people in each circle get up and change places; the outer circle becomes inner, inner circle becomes outer, and then the conversation begins again, wherever people start.

This Socratic Circle goes on for an hour with community members talking about experiences, hopes, fears, and challenges. The energy in the rooms settles into this softness, where everything is focused on the very center of the circles, leaning in to see what is being held in this sacred space of sharing.

Eventually, I call a gentle close to the circles and ask people to pull themselves back to this moment. I ask them to reflect on the experience – what had an impact on them? What did they experience? Reflecting on how this process will work in community as we carry the conversation forward.

There Is No Perfect Structure

One participant immediately speaks up. She has recently returned to one of the communities from years in the city, and she works as a traditional healer. Her body language and voice are strong and certain as she speaks. *"This process will never work for us! Two circles go against all of our teachings. It divides us and forces people into positions they may not want to be in. We can't see each other. This is never going to work. We can't do this."*

After witnessing the hour of sharing and conversation, I'm surprised at the strength of her reaction. I acknowledge her voice and thank her for comment. I ask others to share their experience. An elder looks around the room slowly, considering the faces of community members. She says, *"I wonder if it is good for us to be in the listening chairs. I heard different things when I sat in the outer circle than I heard in the inner circle. I wonder if it is good for us to listen in different ways so we can see our challenges differently. I don't know if this is right or wrong, but I know it helped me listen. And we listen to each other in community."*

Humility. Openness. Courage. Commitment to community, and values. Both speakers demonstrated courage and a deep commitment to community and values. The elder who spoke added a layer of humility and openness to her words that invited learning, participation, and possibility.

I didn't have the answer to whether the Socratic Circle would be right for their community or appropriate for their cultural values. I offer a space for conversation and support the community to determine what will make this important conversation meaningful. It is their conversation and their communities. If I was attached to the design of the process, then I would be centering my experience and perspectives in the process rather than those of the community. The situation makes me think of a saying that often comes up in health care: *"Nothing about me without me."* When we center the people who are impacted in the conversation, holding their needs, experiences, and values at the heart of our conversations, everything has more meaning.

Every Conversation Has a Cultural Context

After the series of workshops were done, we wove the input and wisdom together to identify guiding principles for the conversation about health and wellness that were grounded in cultural values. Noted below are the Seven Grandfather Teachings*, referenced by elders, aligned with community insight about the conversation for this project.

"We need to apply the Seven Grandfathers to this project ourselves. Love them. And what they mean to us. Create a shared understanding of what they mean." – Elder

Seven Grandfather Teachings	What This Means for our Practice of Meaningful Engagement
Nibwaakaawin—Wisdom To cherish knowledge is to know Wisdom. Wisdom is given by the Creator to be used for the good of the people. This word expresses not only "wisdom," but also means "experience," or "intelligence."	**Increased Understanding** – The process will provide people with information so that their understanding of health services and programs is enhanced, and they are more aware and informed as a result of the process. **Increased Ownership** – The conversation and outcome will build ownership for individual, family, and community health and well-being.
Zaagi'idiwin—Love: To know peace is to know Love. Love must be unconditional. When people are weak, they need love the most. This form of love is mutual.	**Care** – The process and resulting health delivery model will demonstrate care and create a sense of togetherness and warmth for all community members and participants.
Minaadendamowin—Respect: To honor all creation is to have respect. All of creation should be treated with respect. You must give respect if you wish to be respected.	**Diversity** – The process will engage more and different people in every community and ensure the voice of health service users and non-users are heard, along with all community members (living on and off reserve). Participants will continuously learn about cultural practices and expectations and make every attempt to adopt their actions accordingly. The process will seek to address power dynamics so as to develop a fair and equitable system.

Aakode'ewin—**Bravery**:
Bravery is to face the foe with
integrity. This word literally means
"state of having a fearless heart."
To do what is right even when the
consequences are unpleasant.

Gwayakwaadiziwin—**Honesty**:
Honesty in facing a situation is
to be brave. Always be honest in
word and action. Be honest first
with yourself, and you will more
easily be able to be honest with
others.

Dabaadendiziwin—**Humility**:
Humility is to know yourself as
a sacred part of Creation. This
word can also mean "compassion."
You are equal to others, but you
are not better. Can also mean
"calmness," "meekness," "gentility"
or "patience."

Time to do it right – Sufficient
time to create and design a
meaningful process and health
delivery model will be taken so
that all participants feel like they
own what is developed.

Address Tensions – The
engagement process will carefully
address and consider tensions,
divides, and fractures within
communities so that people
are able to focus on a common
goal and participate in safety
and comfort in this important
conversation.

**Modeling the Values we Hold
Dear** – Staff, administrators, and
community members will be
encouraged to live the values and
teachings. They will respectfully
"say what they mean" and "do
what they say." There will be no
hidden or self-motivated agendas.

Include All Voices – Dissenting
voices must be encouraged and
made to feel cared for, so that the
engagement process considers
all aspects of the journey in a
constructive way. The focus of
conversation will be without
judgement and blaming, and
about listening to understand.
Staff and administrators will

Debwewin—**Truth:**
Truth is to know all of these things. Speak the truth. Do not deceive yourself or others.

work hard to assume that even perceived negative words/actions were not intended as such, regardless of personal challenges.

Trust and Transparency – The engagement process will build trust, creating an environment where participants and organizations can come together in safety, talk openly, and create new solutions. There will be clear expectations and people will know how their suggestions or input will be used.

*Seven Grandfather Teachings Adapted from University of Michigan, Noongwa e-Anishinaabemjig, The Gifts of the Seven Grandfathers

When we let go of our expectations and assumptions about how things should go, and are open to learning with curiosity and humility, we can create conversations and outcomes that centre people at their heart. That includes aligning with their values, perspectives, and ways of knowing and being.

Reflect and Practice – Using the Socratic Circle

A Socratic Circle is a group conversation process that supports learning, relationships, and embraces high emotion. I've used it in countless situations as a method to embrace the intense concern, anger, fear, worry, or frustration participants are feeling so that it can be understood, and a path created for constructive conversation. The method brings to life the core leadership competency of bringing people together to have important conversations. It creates the container or structure for people to talk about difficult things in ways that deepen understanding, build trust, and strengthen relationships and connection.

Like a spider's web, it creates a strong yet flexible structure for a conversation, and allows connections and dynamics to be visible.

The Socratic Circle was originally created for use in educational settings, with specific focus on building understanding related to literature. I adapted the technique to use in high emotion situations in the public arena and have been teaching and implementing it for decades around the globe. This information focuses on how to lead a Socratic Circle in person; however, you can adapt the process to conduct an online conversation on zoom (instructions for online Socratic Circles are noted following the in-person description).

How Does it Work?

Participants are divided into two concentric circles, both circles with chairs facing into the centre, with generally equal numbers of participants in each circle. The circles create a container for the emotion that models the space that gets created in talking circles, and it intentionally builds deep understanding by forming an outer circle meant only for listening.

The inner circle starts the first conversation based on some prompt questions designed to spark thinking.

The outer circle listens to the conversation to hear and understand what is said, and are also asked to watch for insights, similarities, and meaning. They 'hold the space' for the conversation.

The inner circle can last for ten minutes, or thirty minutes, or somewhere in between depending on the flow of conversation, the topic, and the energy of participants. When circle one ends, the conversation leader calls for a switch, and the inner circle moves to the outer circle to listen, and the outer circle takes the talking chairs in the inner circle.

When both circles have completed discussion, the conversation leader engages both groups in discussion to uncover what stood out for them, what had meaning or insight, where they saw patterns or similarities, or where there may be more that needs to be discussed or considered. The conversation leader can start with hearing from participants in the outer circle, then welcome input from all.

If it feels like there is more to say and the discussion hasn't come to any conclusion or surfaced all that needs to be said, then you can call for another 'wave' of conversation. In this wave you can allow people to self-select who sits in the inner circle, allowing those with more to contribute to hold those chairs. If you take this option, be sure to debrief fully with those in the outer circle before going back to the inner circle at the end.

When Do You Use a Socratic Circle?

Use a Socratic Circle when you want to engage people in powerful thinking, sharing, and learning that does not require a resolution, consensus, or other fixed outcome. Socratic Circles are a great way to ensure participants have ownership of the discussion because they lead and direct it.

The process also encourages equal contributions between participants, and this can be encouraged by tracing the "web" of conversation as participants talk, documenting the pattern and energy of the conversation. At the same time, recorders can document the conversation that is taking place.

Using a Socratic Circle creates a safe and brave place for emotional conversations. It is important to set the stage for the conversation by creating conversation norms, by explaining how the process will work, and acknowledging some of the challenging issues that may be raised.

It is important for all participants to be in the conversation including the organization, stakeholders, and technical experts so that there is a fullness to the conversation, and any of 'us versus them' thinking is diminished.

You can use the Socratic Circle in groups of up to fifty, with the largest circles being twenty-five people in each ring. When you've got more than fifty people, create multiple circles.

SOCRATIC CIRCLE STEP-BY-STEP

STEP 1

Prior to starting the Socratic Circle the conversation leader should identify a number of key questions or inquiries to serve as prompts to kick-start the conversation.

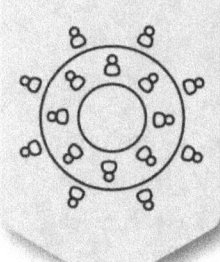

STEP 2

The leader sets up the circle so the chairs are in place in the structure that supports the conversation.

STEP 3

Prior to beginning, participants collect their thoughts related to the prompt questions and write some reflections

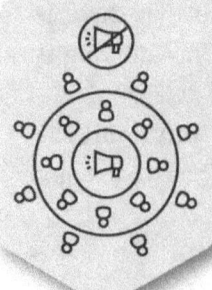

STEP 4

Equal numbers are seated in the inner and outer circles and the conversation leader reminds folks that talking takes place in the inner circle, and listening takes place in the outer circle.

STEP 5

The conversation leader calls time for each session. The leader does not start the conversations, and must remain silent throughout, unless participant safety is at risk.

STEP 6

The conversation leader or another nominated person tracks the conversation using flip charts. Tracking involves identifying the seating position of each participant, and tracing a line from each speaker to the next. This visually demonstrates the flow or 'web' of conversation and how it moved around in the inner circle, tracking the energy of who contributed and where discussed moved. During the outer circle feedback, the leader directs participants' attention to the tracking diagram as a concrete expression of the conversation.

STEP 7

After the first conversation the inner and the outer circles change roles and positions.

STEP 8

At the conclusion of the second outer circle feedback, the leader can lead an open discussion about the process and the content, and pose a question like 'where to from here?' or 'what did you learn?'

Example Prompt Questions

Noted here are a number of example prompt questions used in previous Socratic Circles.

In a long-term conflict situation between a corporation and an indigenous community:

- *What makes a good neighbour?*
- *What do you hope Company X learns about you and your community?*
- *What do you hope to learn about the people at Company X?*
- *What might allow you to work together to have a better relationship?*

In a recovery situation to natural disaster with community workers:

- *How do you make meaning of what has happened and care for yourself when you spend so much time holding other people's needs and emotions?*
- *How do you play a role in contributing to re-building community?*

In a recovery situation to natural disaster with community recovery workers, agencies, and community members:

- *How do we find a way forward to rebuild our communities?*
- *How do we reconcile all the diverse and urgent needs that are calling for attention?*
- *How do we create a recovery process that works for all of us?*

In a high-conflict situation on a health care issue:

- *What are the challenges, struggles, and considerations we need to talk through before moving forward on this issue?*
- *What will we need to learn so that all perspectives can be fully understood, and the complexity of this issue be considered?*
- *What would an informed decision for moving forward look like to you?*

Give the method a try in your next tough conversation and create the space for people to see, hear and understand each other. New connections are made, tensions release and possibility get created for a new way of working and talking together.

Adapting the Process for Online Conversations Using Zoom

The process flows the same way online that it does in person. Here are the adaptations to make:

1. Introduce the process and explain the logistics to people. Get them to visualize two concentric circles, and the role each circle plays: one circle speaking, one circle listening. Once they can visualize the circle, ask them to work through their Zoom settings.

    a. Go to the video tab and click on the drop-down menu to open Video Settings. In video settings, click the bullet that says 'hide non video participants.' This enables the outer circle to become invisible when the inner circle is talking.

    b. Divide participants into two groups, with roughly equal numbers. Remind people of the roles of the inner circle and the outer circle and then read off the names of people in the first group. These people should turn off their videos as you read their name, and they become the outer circle.

    c. Encourage the people left on screen with their videos on to unmute themselves so the conversation can flow.

    d. Post the reflection questions in chat and ask both circles to collect their thoughts and consider the questions.

    e. Then turn off your camera and leave people to the conversation.

    f. After a set period of time, turn your camera back on, thank the first group for their participation, and ask them to mute themselves and turn their cameras off. Welcome the outer circle back in, by asking them to unmute themselves and turn on their cameras. Remind them of their role and turn off your camera so they can begin.

g. When the conversation is over, invite all participants back to the discussion by having everyone turn their camera back on.

Reflect and Practice – Cultural Humility

Cultural humility requires us to hold a mindset of self-awareness and self-criticism and be constantly open to learning. It requires us to center the wisdom and experience of the people we are in conversation with, as experts in their own lives, with the insight to be honoured and valued. Cultural humility allows us to expand our thinking, open to other ways of knowing, perceiving, and interacting with the world.

In order to build your own cultural humility, here are some questions you can ask yourself:

- What am I attached to and certain that I know?
- What if my perspective was wrong for this situation or these people I'm in conversation with?
- What if I stepped back from certainty and got curious? What can I learn here? What might emerge if I open myself to others leading and showing me the way?
- If I am an expert in my own life, what can I learn from these people about their expertise? What perspective, experience and ways of thinking and living can I learn from?
- What work, learning and discovering do I need to be responsible for? How do I do my own work to learn more?
- What wisdom, insights and experience of others can I center in this conversation?

Leadership isn't always about being at the front of the room, carving the path, or setting out the vision. Sometimes leadership is about stepping into humility and curiosity and creating space for others to lead.

Part 2 affirms that life is messy, unpredictable, chaotic, and uncertain. It reminds us that we can make plans, but they can backfire, and we need to refine, adapt and be humble and flexible.

We learn that we are doing difficult and really important work bringing people together into conversation on things that matter, and we need to proceed with care and compassion, contributing to the safety and courage of participants. Drawing on what we learned in Part 1, leading in alignment with our values, clear on our commitments, learning and recovering from failure we can create structures and processes that invite the dynamics and disruption of challenging conversations so that people can learn and grow together.

PART 3

Leadership in the Space Between Us

In Part 3, we go through the deep, muddy, difficult trench that is the emotion of brave, honest conversations so we can work with all that pain and rage. We find meaning and then as we climb out the other side of the trench see the horizon that calls us forward, together.

If you lead in the public arena, your ability to step into the fire of high emotion and embrace the heat of difficult conversations is crucial to shifting the discussion and finding solutions.

CHAPTER 9

From Trauma to Transformation

I'm sitting around a kitchen table with twenty women, squished together companionably drinking tea and eating cookies as the sun streams in the windows of the apartment. We could be a book club, or a mother's group, but we aren't.

We are gathered together so I can lead them through a discussion about how to design a conversation to bring together two hundred more women just like them. Women who hold something in common no one wants to hold, women who have been physically, emotionally, or sexually abused. Women who have gotten back up, found some semblance of safety after fleeing violence, who view the world and the agencies who are meant to support women like them with hesitancy and trepidation.

It turns out that often, there is no one there to help you, and worse, sometimes those who are supposed to help you are the people who actively put you back into danger.

As we drink our tea and eat our cookies, we define our goal; to design a conversation for as many women as we can fit into a room, to share their stories, and to get at the underlying challenges in the system that create barriers to getting support and finding safety. We've called the approach *"every door is an open door."*

Unbeknownst to them, I've got a soft spot for these women and a personal commitment to their quest. A long time ago, I was married for a few years to a man who was emotionally abusive, manipulative, and controlling, and the experience left deep scars on my soul that I struggle with to this day. When they tell their stories and speak of their hopes, the scars in my heart ache with the echo of those times. Those memories propel me forward with extreme motivation and commitment to get this conversation right for them, and all the other women who won't be there.

The Things we Don't Talk About Can Cause us Harm

The things we don't talk about are the things that have the potential to cause us harm. When we shine a light on hard things, they are out in the open, they can be seen and addressed. When we don't talk about things, we keep them hidden in the dark, and like anyone who has nightmares knows, dark hidden things are dangerous, and they grow when you can't see them. This chapter isn't about my past challenges, but it is about how the things we don't talk about can cause us harm, and how if you don't have a support system or support net to fall into like I did, the odds are high that your safety will be imperiled.

I look around at the faces of these beautiful women. These are women from all ethnic backgrounds, cultures, and economic brackets. In their eyes is pain and also commitment. Some are living in shelters with their children, others have restraining orders in place against partners, and some don't leave their homes very often, because the world is dangerous and hard to be in most days. I ask them, *"What do you know for sure will be needed for this to be a conversation that feels safe to women who gather?"*

Supporting the Hardest of Conversations

When I ask the question there is a pause in the room; now we are digging in, beginning to talk about the real stuff and they can feel the air shift around them.

One-woman ventures, "*They will need support. Counsellors. Someone there when they get triggered by the conversation. I will need them there to reach out to when I get triggered.*"

Another woman says, "*We need the space to be nurturing, peaceful, and full of comforts. Good food, soft music, comfortable chairs.*"

These things are doable, some more difficult than others with over two hundred women expected to come, and I note them down.

Then, softly, the woman whose apartment we are in says, "*There should be no men there.*" We all lean in to listen to her. "*My husband is a pillar of the community. Successful, charming, handsome. Everyone loves him. Every morning he would go out into the world and people would heap praise on what a wonderful man he is. Such a good provider, a good father and husband and community member. And every night he would come home and beat me. I've been to the hospital for broken bones and internal damage five times in the last year. The last time I almost died. The police officers who came didn't believe me that it was him. I left with nothing. No money, no savings, just a bag of clothes. To this day I can't be in a room alone with a man, and I don't trust male police officers. I feel like I can't breathe. They look like they are good people, but they could be hiding their monsters in plain sight.*"

What do you say when someone tells you their story?

What do you say when someone shares their secret pain?

This woman, who is a public figure, who has co-hosted fundraisers and community groups, is hiding in this small apartment, with five dead bolts on the door, four stories up because the lower levels run the risk of break-in through the balcony. All of her waking moments are full of heightened anxiety and watchfulness. I just say what I'm thinking. "*Thank you...I don't even know what to say.*"

In this conversation we are planning, we invited all the agencies and organizations who support women experiencing violence so we can look at the system, and identify how to make sure every door is an open door. So that when a woman needs help, every place she turns is prepared to respond with 'yes'. Men work in those organizations too. Supportive, caring men, dedicated to providing the help women need.

What will happen if we invite those groups but tell them those they send must be women?

Making Trade-offs in Challenging Conversations

There is this dance when we talk about difficult things together. The dance between need and hope, between inclusion and equity, between transaction and transformation. The same dance that exists between brave and safe spaces.

In order to highlight the voices of women with lived experience in this conversation, we need to exclude the voices of men who support them.

I hope they will understand this. I think that hope is tied to the echo of my own experience with emotional abuse. There are consequences to setting boundaries and being clear with needs, and sometimes those consequences are negative or unintended. I need to let go of the hope this will be OK and stand in the power that this is the right choice for this conversation, for these women, for now.

In order to raise up voices that have been marginalized we need to centre those voices in the conversation, to the exclusion of all other voices. Sometimes the people whose voices we need to hear don't feel safe enough or brave enough to participate unless we've cleared the space for them. Once those voices are loud, clear, and deeply understood, then other voices can mingle in as a chorus

In order to change how the system works we need to move beyond conversations that look at what is working and what could change, or a focus on the transactional nature of making lists, like identifying three ideas to make things work better. When things are really hard, we yearn for the easy, simple solutions. Complexity, like this situation, requires us to dig deeper, to be present to the pain, heartache, and challenges, to look into them with open eyes and hearts and then to notice how the edges of the system support and protect the status quo. There are no easy answers here.

In order to make change real, to enable transformation, we have to summon the courage and the compassion to be with the hardest things.

To really see and be with them before we move to fixing them. Band-Aids fall off after a while, and the wound can get infected if we haven't cleaned the source of the infection. We don't want band-aid fixes; real change is all that matters.

Transformational Versus Transactional

What is the difference between transformational conversations and transactional conversations?

Sometimes the differences are easy to spot:

- Discussions about to-do lists and errands to run, and who will pick up the children from school versus discussions about how I'm feeling lonely and I miss you, even though we are here in this house together.
- There are conversations that generate lists about deliverables and due dates, timelines, and tasks versus how we leverage our individual strengths to do good work that makes us feel a sense of purpose and accomplishment, like our contributions matter and we have value.
- There are discussions about construction impacts of community infrastructure, and when there will be night work and loud noises, versus conversations about how the baby is up all night, and work from home has become impossible, with no respite from the noise and mental health is suffering in the community.

We know these conversations. We've all been in them. It seems the more stressed and pressured some people get, the more we veer towards transactional discussions as if controlling the details will bring us back to safety and certainty. Instead, they leave us feeling empty, hollow, and hopeless, unseen and undervalued.

In the past, there have been discussions about creating rules, checklists, and procedures about who does what in situations of domestic violence, versus discussions about the stories, experiences, and needs of women who have been victims of violence so we can see the deep patterns and ways of knowing and working that need to shift so everyone has the right to be safe.

Transaction is about short-term exchanges where you get this and I get this, and then we move on. Relationships, trust, and connection are mostly irrelevant. We aren't solving the causes of problems, instead we are treating the symptoms in a superficial way.

Transformation changes things completely, the situation, activities, and our own ways of being are changed permanently into something different because of the conversation or situation. Not just the situation changes; we are different as a result.

Brave, honest conversations enable transformation.

Understanding Emotion

Drawing on the work of Dr. Lisa Feldman Barrett in *Seven and a Half Lessons About the Brain,* in every emotional situation, there is a process your brain and body work through that looks like this:

- Predict
- Simulate
- Interpret / Assign Meaning
- Compare, Learn, and Adapt

Your brain continually predicts and simulates all the sensory inputs from inside and outside your body, so it understands what they mean and what to do about them. This process happens super fast, but we can understand it and work with it if we slow it down. I will share an example to help it make sense.

Here is the situation I recently found myself in: leading a virtual workshop for over seventy participants on a very highly polarized topic. This is the first workshop of a series and I'm a little nervous about how things might go. Setting the tone and stage for the conversation will invite people into the conflict or push them further to their sides.

THE THEORY OF CONSTRUCTED EMOTION

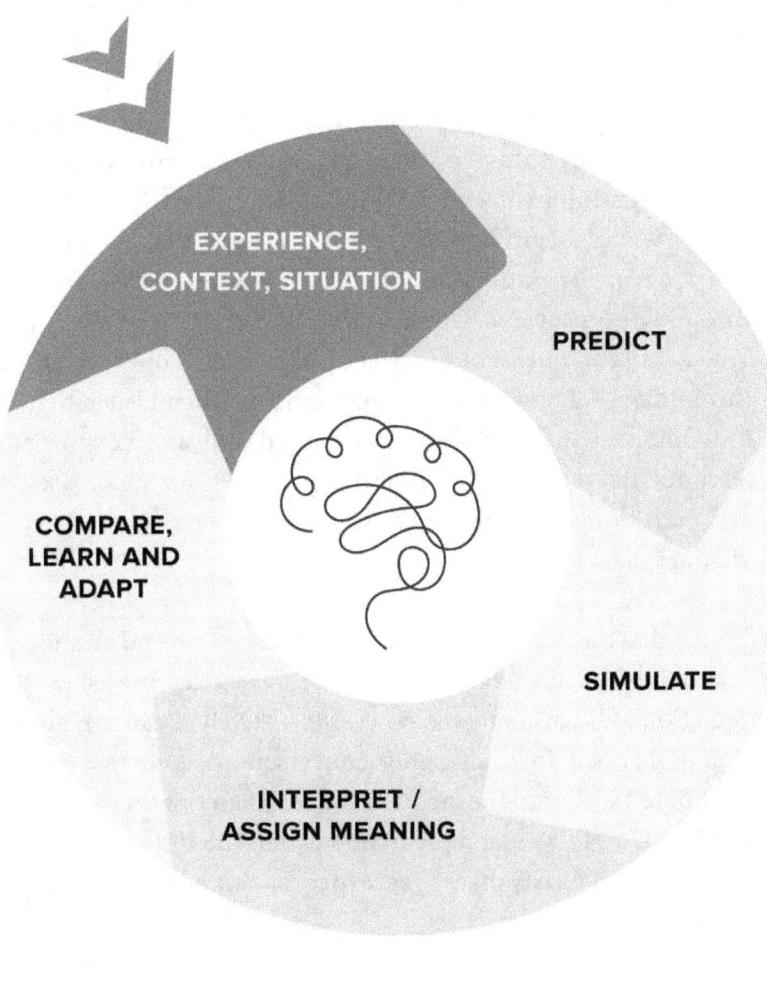

EXPERIENCE, CONTEXT, SITUATION

PREDICT

COMPARE, LEARN AND ADAPT

SIMULATE

INTERPRET / ASSIGN MEANING

WWW.BRAVELYLEAD.COM

Step 1 – PREDICT

Prediction allows us to react quickly. We find ourselves in a situation, and our brain almost immediately assesses what our bodies might need in order to respond to this situation. Our brain's assessment is based on environment, surroundings, and past experience and is a best guess of what might help us in this situation.

- In my example situation, I open the session with an intentional process to slow things down, and model bringing in emotion and thoughtfulness to the conversation. To start I acknowledge territory and begin to say, *"I acknowledge that I work, live, and play on the traditional unceded territories of the Algonquin Anishnaabeg people, and the traditional territory of the Huron-Wendat and Haudenosaunee (Iroquois) peoples."* I only get halfway through my acknowledgement of territory, when I learn that one individual in the workshop is unmuted and as I acknowledge territory he yells into his microphone, *"Oh, for fucks sake not this bullshit again!"* His voice is loud and reverberates into the virtual space.

I can predict that this is a disaster, and it is embarrassing and humiliating for me, and that I've misjudged how to start this virtual workshop. This first prediction will have one outcome. Alternatively, I can predict that these things happen in challenging conversations, and his outburst means I should be alert to the fact that the real conversation has begun, and all will be OK. This second prediction will have a different outcome. Both these predictions rely on my past experiences, and the environment and context I find myself in.

Step 2 – SIMULATE

The brain gives the body what it thinks it needs to address the situation, changing physiology, sending chemicals like adrenaline, cortisol, dopamine, and other resources to the body to ensure it can respond.

- In my example situation, when Fred (let's call him that) yells in the middle of my welcome to the conversation I get sweaty and flushed. I can feel my heart beating faster and my belly churning. I can feel the cortisol and adrenaline in my system preparing me to be alert and respond.

Step 3 – INTERPRET / ASSIGN MEANING

This is where emotion comes in. Based on our past and environment, what we are experiencing in our body, we interpret the experience as emotion. We can interpret our body flooded with adrenaline and cortisol as fear and anxiety, or we can interpret the same experience as excitement and anticipation.

We have some control over how we interpret our emotions if we can raise our awareness of what we are experiencing.

- In my example situation, I interpret the situation as 'game on' and 'we've begun' so that I'm fully present and alive to what is happening. This is a high stakes conversation and there are bound to be high emotions throughout. It isn't bad that Fred expressed his frustration and cynicism; instead, it is a marker of the intensity of this moment. I make light of the situation and say, *"Fred, I just want you to know that you are unmuted, and we all heard your frustration. I'm going to finish what I was saying and then it turns out I've picked the perfect reading to open our session – it is about humility, inviting all of us to be as curious as we can be in this challenging discussion."*

Now all of this processing happens too fast for me to witness, but I've slowed it down for you.

We can slow it down for ourselves too if we can get curious in the moment between simulation and interpretation and simply ask ourselves *what is going on here?* Remember that I could also have interpreted this moment as embarrassment and humiliation, experiencing shame that I'd chosen wrong and failed the group.

The more we slow it down and the more we give ourselves optional emotions to choose from, the more our brain can apply those possibilities to the situations we experience. From our interpretation comes meaning, and that carries into the emotion we experience, and the emotion in the space between us.

Step 4 – COMPARE, ADAPT, AND LEARN

Our brain compares the prediction it made to the experience we had in order to see if it needs to change the way it responds in future situations.

We then adapt our experience and reconcile whether fear was the emotion or perhaps excitement was called for instead, applying that learning to future situations.

- In my example situation my brain now has additional information for the future. This situation might require a little less cortisol and adrenaline in the future; it's a reason to be fully present, but not a reason to be plunged into humiliation and shame and need to hide.

Prepare Yourself

If you have an upcoming brave, honest conversation you can prepare yourself by working through the prediction process so that when your brain tells your body to be prepared, it has choices for how to respond.

Let me give you another example of how to apply this thinking *in preparation* for a difficult situation, rather than in the moment. I'm preparing myself for a process to support trainers of an organization to learn to teach a new curriculum I have been part of developing. I'm feeling nervous, hesitant, judged, and a little tense about the process.

I'm predicting that some people in this group of trainers believe they have little to learn about this new curriculum, especially from me. I'm predicting that they believe they are the experts and don't want or need guidance in these new courses. I'm even predicting that some of them will judge the new curriculum harshly and find it lacking. I'm predicting that they will do things to resist, slow, or even damage the new curriculum in order to protect their own interests and ego. I've got stories in my own head circling around based on these predictions.

The impact of those predictions is that I believe the program may be unsuccessful, and that I will be unsuccessful as a leader.

I'm basing this prediction on previous experience with some of this group; that they have in the past been highly critical of change, lobbying for the status quo and their own interests over the interests of the organization, and that they see themselves as foremost experts who don't have anything else to learn. My predictions make me feel like everyone will respond this way, but the reality is that not all of them will. It is more likely that a few of them will match my predictions, and my direct previous experience with those few of them is contributing to my prediction of how things will go.

I know that I want something different than the outcome of this negative prediction. I want this program to be a space of learning and growth for everyone. A space where people can play, share, contribute, and feel confident and prepared to deliver the new curriculum when they complete the process. I want this process to be a space where those who are uncomfortable with the changes, or who are judging the process feel welcome to participate as well. I want to honour all of their expertise and guide them to see what is new and has changed too. I want to be open, committed to a collaborative approach to bring new curriculum into the world, and also welcome input, changes, and suggestions from this group of committed professionals. I want to be open to people making the choices that are right for them – including participating in the program or not participating in the program.

Predict Something Different

If I want something different, I need to predict something different.

I need to predict that to create a space of learning and growth means that I have something of value to offer as a guide for this journey. I need to draw on other previous experience of coaching groups, mentoring colleagues, and leading training successfully to create a place of play, sharing, and contribution.

I need to predict that working together on the curriculum and the program will be richer because of our contributions, and recall all the experiences I have of doing exactly that.

When I draw on these other experiences to predict something different, I feel differently. I feel excited and prepared, anticipating the journey ahead in a positive way.

This positive orientation will allow me to respond differently in the moment when the event happens and prepares my brain for responses.

Above the Line and Below the Line: Emotion on a Scale

Emotions determine what we care about and what motivates us. They connect us to others and give us the courage to step into fear to achieve our goals, to celebrate achievements, to be empathetic and caring with those around us. They allow us to inspire, encourage, and empower others to be their best in pursuit of a shared goal.

Emotions are energy in motion, and the energy they generate impacts your inner state, the state that others experience, and the space around the issue you are discussing, rippling to affect others on the periphery and connect to related issues.

Some emotions are expansive, and some emotions are constrictive, and there is a line that differentiates this shift in energy; the line is courage.

Courage is a catalyst emotion that crosses the line from what was, to what is, from constricting to expansive, that shifts the energy and allows different meaning and interpretations.

Emotions above the courage line allow for creativity, innovation, problem-solving, relationships, trust, connection, humour, and possibility. Emotions below the line are focused on certainty, protection, defense, control, or hiding. Above-the-line and below-the-line emotions both have wisdom and insight for us, but the meaning they give us, and the results we can achieve are vastly different.

The act of naming emotion reduces its intensity and creates an observer mind, which allows the person in a high arousal state to begin to interpret their experience and start to find meaning.

ASCENDANCY OF EMOTIONS

There is an ascendancy to emotions. They impact the energy inside of you and between you and others. Emotion = energy in motion. What wisdom or insight is there for you in what you are feeling?

HOPE, LOVE, TRUST, GRATITUDE

EMPATHY, COMPASSION, KINDNESS

FREEDOM, AUTONOMY

WELL-BEING, CONTENTMENT, HAPPINESS

PASSION, THRILL, EXCITEMENT

CREATIVITY, INNOVATION, OPENNESS, ACCEPTANCE

COURAGE, BRAVERY, COMMITMENT TO CHANGE

ANGER, RAGE

FRUSTRATION, CYNICISM, IMPATIENCE

APPREHENSION, ANXIETY, WORRY

FEAR, TERROR

SHAME, GUILT, BETRAYAL, HURT, GRIEF

HOPELESSNESS, LONELINESS, DESPAIR

WWW.BRAVELYLEAD.COM

If we improve everyone's emotional literacy by asking people to name the emotion they are experiencing, and to share the impact of that emotion on them, we are creating a conversational space where meaning can be identified, and where a shift is possible.

Perhaps the most difficult thing about working with emotion is to get over our own socially programmed conditioning that talking about feelings at work or in public is wrong, shameful, or unprofessional. If we can let go of these inaccurate assumptions that suggest emotions are illogical or inappropriate, we build our capacity to make meaning. Because we all have emotions, right?

Reflect and Practice – Building Your Comfort With Emotion

Building your comfort and capacity to be with your own emotions, whether they are above or below the line, allows you to come home to yourself.

When you are powerfully living and leading from your own home, you can connect with others when they are feeling deeply, and together find a way forward that is grounded in meaning and purpose.

When you are connected with others you are more creative and innovative, and able to solve problems. It's counterintuitive; talking about your feelings helps you be more effective and perform better.

The questions to ask yourself are:

- Can you do the uncomfortable thing and talk about emotions?
- How can you resist the urge to make the discomfort you are feeling mean that this is bad or wrong, and instead get curious about what it is teaching you instead?
- Can you sidestep the judgement that lets you feel right, and be open to the wonder of what you might learn?
- Can you step into the fire of emotion and stay there?
- What insights can we draw from this situation?
- How do we move forward with our fear and also our hope?

- Can you embrace the emotion and make all of it all right – which also draws other people above the line?
- Can you consider what it would be like if we worked together to meet our collective needs rather than blaming or shaming each other?
- Can you imagine what it might be like to work through the feelings and get to the heart of the issue, enabling problem solving and new ideas to emerge?

When you do this, you create a shift, lean into integration and wholeness, and get better results.

CHAPTER 10

There Is a Crack in Everything – That Is How the Light Gets In

There are experiences and moments that change your world. All the stories matter, but this one is hard to write. I've talked about this experience in speeches, but when you speak from a stage or tell a story to deepen the learning of others in a workshop you skirt over details and the deep, hidden pain in your secret heart.

In my own secret heart.

So here we go.

I was hired by a provincial power company to "transform ninety years of conflict" between them and an indigenous community, as if I could wave my magic wand, sprinkle some pixie dust, and undo decades of the impacts of colonization and the ninety years of harm and damage that went with them.

I had told the company that the transformation would take a decade or more, and what I could perhaps do, with the community's commitment and support, is to carve a new path for the company and the community to walk together.

It is a small, remote community in the north of Canada, with about twenty-five hundred residents, set among bogs and forest, on the shores of a river. The roads are impassable at different times of the year, so we had been flying in and out onto a dirt air strip for over six months. We stayed a week or two at a time, getting to know people, building trust and relationships slowly, and holding space for what a different future might look like between the company and the community.

Heartache Is Everywhere

Two days before we were due to fly in for a ten-day visit we learned that two children in the community had just died by suicide. I got a sick, weak feeling in my stomach and I was heartsick for the community. Should we go? Would we be intruding on their grief? Could we be of service? I reached out to some community members and elders; they said to come. Perhaps we could host a meal that would support the community to come together. Perhaps we could set up the space to talk, and people could come and share their grief, fear, or anger sitting together with a cup of tea.

The loss of these two lives was directly tied to the ninety years of harm we were trying to understand and chart, and if we could be of service then we would go.

My Own Heart Is Aching

What I didn't share with everyone on my team, was that my teenage daughter was struggling with depression and anxiety and had been for months. She was seeing a therapist, and we were modifying her medication trying to find the right balance. Those are details – the experience was different. She was weeping in her room more often than not, missing school, lost to the pit of despair that had opened up beneath her.

She had support – my husband, ex-husband and his partner, extended family, friends, and doctors. I agonized over whether I should go north or not. What was the right thing to do? We talked and talked about it as a group of parents. Do I stop working because my child is struggling? When do I stay and when do I go? In the end, we decided I should go. So, I packed my bags, kissed my children, held my daughter a little longer than normal, and hoping for the best, I flew to this small, remote community struggling with their own tragedies and pain.

Looking back now I don't know if there was a different decision I could have made at that moment.

How do you know what the right choice is?

Sometimes there are no right choices, just really hard ones. We landed in the community and held space in the community centre and the church basement, serving coffee, eating meals, sitting in small circles and at tables with whoever needed a space to gather, to talk, and to connect.

Two days into this hard, open-hearted work with the community I got a phone call.

My daughter had just tried to kill herself. She had been admitted to the psychiatric ward of the children's hospital. They weren't allowing her to receive calls from anyone.

I was in this remote community, where the plane wasn't coming back for another week and my daughter was in the hospital. I was in a community that had just had two children die by suicide, and my child had tried to take her life.

I was consumed by heartache, grief, guilt, and anxiety. What kind of mother did this make me? Hadn't she told me she was suffering? Hadn't I decided she had support and I was needed elsewhere? Is this why she did what she did? I couldn't even talk to her, couldn't tell her my heart was with her, that I loved her, that I was sorry. What kind of parent makes the choice I made? I was sure this choice made me the world's worst mother. Was this my fault? Would my child be OK? Please let her be OK.

I talked to my husband and other family members. They were there supporting her, visiting when they were allowed to, the hospital was working on stabilizing her health, and she was being well cared for. I couldn't do anything for her from afar, so what could I do? I couldn't leave the community to go to her until the plane came back. So, I was here, in this most challenging of moments, thousands of miles away from my hurting child.

I made a choice of what I could do at that moment. I wish I could tell you it was the right choice, or that I've got advice for you if you ever find yourself in a similarly awful circumstance. But really, who knows? Sometimes there are no good choices, just hard ones.

You Always Have a Choice

Since I was confined to the community for another week, I knew I could stay in our lodgings, and send my team to work with the community, and nurse my tender, anxious, fearful heart.

I could go out into the community and tell them what I was dealing with, because it would be obvious that I was messy all around my edges.

I chose neither of those options; staying in would make the minutes go slower and I'd be doing no good to anyone. Telling people of my pain would take away from theirs, and my child was alive while theirs were not, and there was no way I wanted to add to their burden.

So instead, I leaned into my tender, fragile heart and went out into the community and held space. I listened, I cried with them, I held hands, I sat beside people while they talked.

Lessons to Carry Forward

I learned a small lesson those days that impacted every conversation I led going forward.

When we lead from where we are, when we are vulnerable and open, and meet people where they are rather than where we want them to be, the space we create contains the seeds of healing, for us and for them.

When we can touch our own pain, we can be with other's heartache.

When we lead from the place of our greatest vulnerability, the space we create allows others to bring their whole selves.

When we are in service to something outside of ourselves, despite, or perhaps because of our own challenges, we meet the moment and what it needs from us.

I flew home a few days later and went to the hospital from the airport. I have had a decade since that moment to learn the lessons my daughter has taught me about how to be with someone when they are in the pit of despair, when there is nothing for you to fix, when the problem isn't yours to solve.

Sometimes love isn't enough to heal someone.

Sometimes, the burden is theirs to carry, and you can only walk beside them when you can.

These are lessons I learned over many years. In those early moments I was racing in with all my mama bear energy to fix things that I couldn't fix.

The seeds of my belief that the leadership the world needs now is grounded in an open heart, from a deep compassion, sprouted in this moment, planted by my dear daughter and the beautiful people of this small, struggling community.

Conversations That Lean Towards Healing and Transformation

In the song "Anthem," Leonard Cohen urges us to let go of our desire for perfection and recognize that there is a crack in everything, and through that crack the light comes in. It is a metaphor for the beauty and wisdom that comes from pain, challenge, and difficulty, if we allow it.

The song is the perfect anthem for this work of brave, honest conversations. We need to let go of perfection as it's not possible, and not as rich and beautiful as the messiness that comes with being fully human. Believing that wholeness requires us to be with our pain and our possibility at the same time, that the cracks that break us are the places where we shine the brightest give us strength and capacity to embrace emotion. Embracing emotion is the place to start in conversations that gently lead us on a path to healing ourselves and the breaks in the space between us.

In order to create space for transformational conversations that lead us towards healing, consider:

Meeting people where they are rather than where you want them to be. When we initiate a brave, honest conversation we often prepare with the end in mind – how there will be deeper understanding and more connection when we are finished. We see the person or people across from us in that end state, and so we begin urging them where we want them to be. I wish that worked, but in my experience, it almost always backfires into a feeling of manipulation, coercion, or disrespect. When we are attached to the outcome, we are in the future, not the present. To be in a brave, honest conversation we must be fully in the present moment, open to what is here, what is emerging, what is inside of us and inside of others, alive to the space between us.

Noticing where there is tension that requires attention. You know it's there even if you don't acknowledge it – your body can feel the tension of the emotion in your tight shoulders, churning stomach, sweaty palms, fluttering heart, or pounding head. Listen to the signals your body is sending. Know that when tension is present, it is time to pay attention, get ready because the journey has already begun.

Bearing witness to the courage, struggle, and energy. Whatever the struggle is, it's brave to feel into it, to acknowledge its presence, to let it see the light of day. It's an honour for someone to show us their vulnerable shadows and invite us to witness the energy that has led them to this moment in their journey. Treat emotion as a gift that lights the path to making meaning, learning, growth, and transformation.

Inquiring with deep compassion. Ask questions that create the space for curiosity. Questions that begin 'how' or 'what,' and questions that allow us to create the whole where there is darkness and light like: What wisdom or insight does your grief have for you? What might your loneliness or despair say to your closest friend right now if they were listening deeply? What change or need is your anger or fear pointing you to? These are the questions that allow us to be sad and grateful, frustrated, and hopeful, afraid, and loving, all at the same time.

Seeing surface patterns, wisdom, and experience. What people say and what they mean can be different. What we offer and what we understand can be far apart. Sometimes we don't even know what is beneath the surface inside of us or between us until we have begun the conversation. It is in the seeking together that the real meaning and insights surface. Watch for them and don't go too quickly to a conclusion. What is here? What is not here? What does it point to? What are we missing? Look for patterns and clues so transformation is possible. Too quick and you will find yourself in the cycle of transaction.

Recognizing this takes time and repetition. Brave, honest conversations are a life's work in your family, organization, and community. One conversation isn't transformation – it is a first step on a long journey.

Choose the Energy You Bring

The best definition of emotion is that it is energy in motion. It creates a current within us, between us, and around us. That energy can be light-hearted, loving, and full of possibility. Or it can be darker, heavier, sluggish, and heavy, constricting our thoughts and actions, and narrowing the space between us. That energy affects us personally, and it is alive in the interaction between us, a force of its own.

Think of the rawest, most difficult, painful conversations you have had with others – the weight of those discussions is heavy down the phone line, across the dinner table, in the meeting room. That saying "you can cut the tension with a knife" is evidence of that energy in motion.

The same is true of the most beautiful conversations you have had with others – the first time you told your partner you loved them, and it was reciprocated, the moment of your child's birth, the laughter and hilarity of shared family jokes and memories – there is a sweet, precious, lightness in the space that expands between us. We feel light, open, and possible; this becomes part of the moments we remember – not just how we felt, but what infused the moment like the smell of spring lilacs on a warm evening.

To lead and participate in brave, honest conversations we must intentionally harness the energy in motion within us, and between us. That means we must build our capacity to be with emotion ourselves, as the greater our own capacity to be with our feelings, the greater our capacity to be with the feelings of others.

We must also build our skills to intentionally bring the energy to the conversation that will serve the moment and the people in it. Sometimes that means bringing the same emotion that is in the space, and other times it means bringing something totally different that will enable the shift that creates the space for transformation.

For example, if you are grieving, I can bring my own despair and sadness and sit with you. That might be what you need, to sink into it and give yourself over to it for a time so the depth of your loss is known. Or I could bring love and compassion and sit with you. We could celebrate the previous joys and memories you hold dear; we could be grateful for all life has given (and taken from) us. We could honour the grief by living. Can you feel the difference in the energy?

When we are intentional about what is inside us, what is in the space between us, and what will serve others and the conversation, we plant the seeds for the garden of transformation.

Reflect and Practice – Preparing for an Emotional Conversation

As you prepare yourself for a conversation laden with emotion, ask yourself:

- **How do I want to show up?** What energy and emotion inside of myself can I be in touch with at this moment?
- **What am I committed to?** What grounds me and allows me to stand firmly when the winds of emotion blow strongly? What do I believe in that will serve this moment and these people?
- **What impact do I want to have?** What energy will serve this conversation and lift it towards transformation? What can I bring that meets people where they are at and stretches them one step further?

When you know the answers to those questions you are ready to step into the storm.

CHAPTER 11

Yearning for Change in a World of Despair

I'm walking the circle, slowly and methodically moving around the inner edge of the circle, looking in the eyes of each person gathered in the community hall. They've been in conversation for a full day already and I'm calling them into a circle on the morning of day two, settling the energy, and transitioning them into today's conversation.

I'm feeling grateful for the magic of this place, this wooden structure set in an old growth forest, nestled on the shores of a small island off the coast of British Columbia, Canada. I've slept in a guest house in the woods and woken to birdsong and the smell of cedar. I know from experience that it is on day two of conversation when the cracks start to show.

Like the Leonard Cohen song "Anthem," the cracks are where the light shines through. I know this from experience, and I also know that this gathering of people doesn't know that yet. They've slept on the discussion from yesterday, and they are leaning in, eager for connection and excited to get going. They think they've done the hard work already, and expect that today will be all fun, smiles, and friendship, full of unicorns and rainbows.

I'm walking the circle, looking deeply into the eyes of each person, channeling my faith in their ability to have these hard conversations, and sending that energy to them. I've been brought here to help this community relearn how to talk together about really hard things, as conflict has been rising between community members and there are rifts and divides along community lines on issues of people without housing, access to water, land use, and reconciliation.

I say, *"I know you are all feeling positive, connected, and expansive this morning. You've done some really hard work already, building your leadership muscles by talking together about the things that are really important in this community. Now I want to ask you to consider, what was left unsaid yesterday? What secret yearnings, deep wounds, judgments, and assumptions might you be carrying about others? What do you need to clear here today so you can be ready to move forward together?"*

Take a Deep Breath and Crack Everything Open

To me, the room feels like it has taken a deep shaky breath. I can feel the walls heaving with what has not yet been said. I know it just takes one person to be brave, to be honest enough to crack open the real rifts and challenges in this community, so the whole group can work with it before they move to healing.

I know it's coming, even though they are looking around at each other, uncomfortable, hoping that perhaps there is nothing hard to be said and they can hold on to the familiar, safe status quo where nothing changes, and nothing requires the pain of growth.

Then one woman abruptly stands and her chair tips backwards with a crash that echoes in the room. The whole room goes silent, in the way that silence can signal foreboding. With an angry, flushed face, and a shaking voice, she shouts, *"I have been belittled and ridiculed for years! No one listens to me! Everyone thinks I'm crazy! I'm not crazy – I'm the only person on this island who cares about all the living creatures, including you! I want you to know that those of you who hunt should be tracked down and shot like the animals you murder for your own needs. You know who you are!"*

It has begun.

I let the room settle – you can see the shock, anger, frustration, and defensiveness swirling in bright colours like a kaleidoscope in the middle of the circle. I take a deep breath, plant my feet firmly to ground myself and say, *"Thank you, Brenda* for being brave enough to share your deepest fears and thoughts with all of us. I would ask that we go around the circle and share how you were impacted by what was said or share your own words that are calling to be said. I want to be clear – I am NOT asking for you to respond to Brenda, but to dig in and go deeper – what is here for you now, and what do you need to surface?"*

(*not her real name)

When we Talk About the Real Stuff we Really See Each Other

I wish I could tell you it was this beautiful circle of sharing, and the healing began right away, but that isn't the way it works.

I wish I could say that we can say hard, hurtful things to each other, and we can step over them to forgive and move forward right away and get down to business, but that isn't the way it works.

I wish it was possible we could all have the emotional intelligence and the peaceful loving nature of the Dalai Lama and kindly open our vulnerable hearts to each other, but most of us aren't like that when things matter most, and our tender hearts are bruised.

I wish we could go from this moment to the end, but first we have to stand in the fire. It is so deeply messy, uncomfortable, and hard, and when you are in the middle of it, sometimes it feels like it might never end. I know that when I am in it I want to curl into a ball or just walk out of the room. So I'm holding the space for this group to stay between those extremes, to withstand the discomfort and see each other without projecting the discomfort outwards to make each other wrong.

Believe it Is Possible to Get Through This Well

I know from experience that on the other side of this mess there is something more possible, more expansive, than they had before, if they can only keep with it. I know this day will end with the seeds of forgiveness, healing, and connection planted in rich soil. I know that if they do this hardest thing, where all the stories they are telling themselves, all the pain and judgement is brought to the surface, and they find their way to loving each other's humanity, they will be twice as strong and resilient as when they walked into this room this morning.

I know they don't know this yet though, so I have to know it for them.

Conversation as the Conduit

The conversation is the conduit to connection, deeper understanding, stronger trust, and relationships. Without the conversation those things are not possible. Without those things, we can't solve anything, but with them we can address any problem we face in our lives, organizations, or communities.

There is an ebb and flow to these conversations, like waves in the ocean, that can happen if you make room for the discussion to flow, contained within a structure.

Conversation Needs a Container or Structure

In a similar way to the use of the Socratic Circle, the structure is the method, technique, questions, and physical space we set up for a difficult conversation. If we sit in circles so we can see each other fully, rather than on two sides of a table like adversaries, we are more likely to deepen understanding. If there is someone, (or multiple people) who lead and guide others through the toughest parts, providing comfort and care that the difficult discussions are all right, they can keep going.

This is about the roles we play naturally, and the roles we assign to support the structure of the conversation. If we use methods and techniques designed as containers that empower agency and choice, facilitate deliberation on complex issues together, and ask questions that strengthen understanding, we create a structure that allows us to get through the chaos to find meaning and transformation. This structure is part of the tools, skills, knowledge, and ways of being, leading, and facilitating challenging conversations.

Riding the Waves of Emotion in the Conversation

The ebb and flow of conversations crests up, with heightened emotion, and the energy of what people are feeling rushes into the room, touching and getting everyone wet like waves surging on shore.

Like a wave, the energy of the emotion can't be sustained indefinitely, and it will inevitably recede if you have a structure in place that allows it to dissipate. If you don't have a structure in place, it can continue to rise, sometimes with destructive force.

Intervene to Channel the Energy of the Emotion

Considering how you intervene in the chaos, to disrupt, redirect, or channel the energy of emotion is how the wave recedes.

You can do simple things like calling a break, using humour to shift and surprise the intensity, changing the physical space by standing on a chair, speaking loudly, and getting people to move to a new location.

You can call for silence and reflection, ask people to think first and then speak about what is most important to them, ask them to grapple with the needs of others, or go deeper into complexity.

Structure is the antidote to chaos.

Be careful though; too much structure will create chaos as people push back on feeling manipulated and controlled.

Ride the waves, rather than try to control them.

Once you've guided one wave to recede, know that as long as people are in the conversation about the real, important thing, another one will come soon enough. Over time, the waves of emotion and chaos get smaller and the winds of connection and understanding blow through the space, until suddenly the energy is above the line and people are creatively finding solutions to problems that seemed intractable and insurmountable.

These waves are true for the group in conversation with their hearts on their sleeves, and it is true too for you, as a leader of some of the most important conversations people will have. These waves happen in the conversations in our lives, our organizations, and in community like this one.

Holding Space Is a Leadership Competency

"Retreat three is a week of learning to lead from nothing."

A number of years ago I participated in a yearlong leadership program with the Coaches Training Institute. There were four weeklong retreats over the course of the year, each of them with a theme. Retreat one was about leading self, retreat two was about leading others, and retreat three was about leading from nothing. As I headed into retreat three, I was thinking; What is going to happen here? What are we going to learn about NOTHING? How do you lead from NOTHING?

And yet here I was. I thought I would be able to connect my experience of leading tough conversations and 'holding space' for people in dialogue to what I would learn in this retreat. With my work focused on high emotion and conflict I was fairly sure I knew what holding space was, and how to do it. Turns out I had a lot more to learn.

I've used the words 'holding space' for years, and I put my hands out in front of me with palms open to the sky when I say those words and I can literally feel the weight of the emotion, yearning, hopes, and conversation I hold in my hands. The idea is nebulous, intangible, and I can't explain to people how to do it, or what to do with the space once they've held it.

The more work I do in creating shifts through dialogue and brave honest conversations, the more I realize I have so much more to learn. Twenty-five+ years of experience is a drop in the bucket of what there is to know about the power of this work to change people's lives.

What Is Holding Space Anyway?

Why is it a leadership skill? Leaders inspire others to make choices or take actions towards a goal or vision. Leaders work with others to make change happen, whatever kind of change they believe is needed. Leaders empower others to be better. Everyone has the potential to be a leader.

In order to do that, leaders need enormous self-awareness, authenticity, and deep commitment to their beliefs. Leaders need to create from others, to draw from them potential and possibility, and to lean into others as well, to bring new ideas to life that couldn't exist without the energy of two or more working together. Leading from nothing becomes an important skill when it allows leaders to read, understand, and work with the energy and possibility in the space around people and issues, and the space within themselves.

To make the concept less nebulous, think about a few tangible examples:

- Reading the tension between people or groups.
- Understanding that there is something that needs to be said that no one has the courage to say.
- Following an urge to ask a question that seems off topic because your intuition tells you there is another issue underlying the one you are talking about with people.
- Staying with the uncomfortable conversation in gentle, loving ways so people can withstand the challenge and see the truth and possibility begin to emerge.
- Welcoming in humanity, connection, and feeling, even when everyone is more comfortable talking about topics, issues, and the agenda.
- Seeing the bigger picture, and how one issue connects to another issue in a system and bringing that into focus.
- And clearing the space inside you so you can be receptive and aware of what is happening with others.

Leading From Nothing Allows the Future to Emerge

After spending a week in the woods in this leadership program learning to lead from nothing, I began to see insights on holding space, and leading from what you cannot see. I start to consciously apply them to work, and deepen my thinking about holding space.

- **Create a stake and live in it:** When you are leading a session/event and interacting with others it's really important to have something to ground yourself. I like to ask myself three questions: What do you believe? What do you bring? What are you in service to? Let's look at an upcoming situation—I am leading a workshop soon with sixty leaders in the healthcare field, talking about conflict and controversy with the community related to hospital closures. I BELIEVE that when I am courageous and open-hearted, I can serve others. I BRING my depth of experience. I am IN SERVICE TO their growth as leaders in connecting with and serving their communities. Put it all together and my stake is, *"When I am courageous and openhearted, I bring my experience in service of stronger connections and better care."*

  This stake will serve me in creating a space for learning, deep conversation, and growth. It's the reason WHY I'm doing this work. This belief will hold me courageous and committed to the people, the content, and to the space I create. I try to create a stake for every day, every event, and every interaction to ground me. When I forget to do it, I can tell right away why I'm blown off course by the winds.

- **Step into what arises, whatever it is:** In this work we talk so often about 'naming the elephant' when you can feel the unsaid things stomping around the room that need to come out. Notice the energy in the space between people—what does it feel like? Is it crunchy or smooth? Is tension building or easing? Did the tone or emotion in the discussion suddenly change? Did you say something and trigger something for someone else? Watch for and be aware of everything that is happening, far beyond what gets said or how people move their bodies. It is in the energy of the emotion that you will find insight. It takes courage to step in when you don't know or can't name what is there. Centre yourself, and move forward to whatever arises, knowing you are in service to the group.

- **Recognize that the space inside of you is as important as the space around you:** You need to be clear, open, and committed in order to lead from nothing and hold the space for others. That means doing your own work in terms of self-awareness, calmness, and an open heart. Whatever it takes to manifest that for yourself, it will need to be a regular practice in order to build the muscles that support your strength in this work. For me this includes exercise, meditation, journaling, and time in nature. The clearer and more open I am, the better I am able to serve.

In addition, I'm learning that this practice also helps me recover faster and more fully when I'm thrown off balance by challenges, difficulties, or my own reactions to situations. When I don't create time or space for myself, I'm less capable of this work.

- **Open up your senses**: Deep awareness of what is in the space is required. Listen with your ears and your heart, see with your eyes and your intuition, feel with your skin and your emotional radar, taste with your imagination and your physical reaction to the space. It's easy to become caught up in the content, issues, and details and forget what is most important. It's easy to get caught up in your own head wondering if you are credible enough, knowledgeable enough, or thinking about the next thing you need to accomplish.

  I've taken to spending time in nature listening to the wind blow in the trees, watching the spaces between the leaves, watching the feeling of the air as it moves beneath the wings of the birds. Sounds like a lot of 'woo woo' doesn't it? What I do know is that doing this has strengthened my awareness and ability to read what is there, AND what is coming. It's helped me serve my team, clients, and participants because I am fully aware of, and connected to what is in the space around the issues or content we are discussing. Our conversations are richer, more nuanced, and results are improving. So go spend an hour staring at some blades of grass and see what emerges.

- **Connect, connect, connect:** Leading from nothing and holding the space means a *constant* checking in with what is happening for the people, and in the space to see what is emerging. You can't check in once at the beginning, or a few times if things get challenging, and think you're really holding space. It's more like turning on the lights and leaving them on in the background as you go about your activities. Because the lights are on you can see things you need to see while you're leading the conversation. If you don't keep the lights on, things get dim, and you only see what is right in front of you. It takes a lot of energy to always have the lights on, but the outcomes are brighter, clearer, and everyone can see the way forward when you exercise this skill.

- **Seek awareness of how your leadership impacts the space in intended and unintended ways:** You've got a stake to ground you, you are centered and open, you are practising awareness, and checking in to connect with what is going on, so everything will go well, right? Yes, and also, no. There is no certainty in how things will go because you are dealing with real, live energy that comes from people, situations, and places.

  You may impact the space in the way you intend. And you may also have unintended impacts—like when people tune out, turn off or react negatively. Enhancing your ability to read these impacts, to step into them as they emerge, and to seek feedback on what has happened will serve you and others. For example, when I get frustrated that people can't see what I can see and I try to tell them how to move forward, I lose them instead of making the way clearer.

  They tune out or react to me being frustrated. That's an unintended impact, because I'm in service to helping them find the way forward on the issues they are dealing with.

  However, once I follow the frustration urge and step into that, I'm no longer serving others, instead I'm serving myself, then I'm thrown off my stake.But if I can say to the group, *"I'm feeling frustrated here, and I know that means I'm acting forcefully. I'm eager for you to find the right way forward for YOU, rather than follow MY way forward. Let's begin again. What do we need to do to regroup?"* Then I've noticed and named my unintended impact. Every day we have intended impacts, and unintended impacts. The key is in building your awareness, stepping in, and beginning again in service to the group and the conversation.

Inviting Light Into the Darkness

"What is your relationship to joy?"

That question was voiced a few years ago by a colleague as we were talking about working with high emotion. In my practice, I've got a friendly relationship with some of those intense and difficult emotions, fear, anger, grief, and anxiety. It's not often that joy, happiness, or excitement is present in my work so the question made me pause and reflect.

I've always just assumed that I've got a positive relationship with joy and happiness because those are the 'good' emotions, and what could be hard about being with those? In my life with family and friends I can point to lots of moments of joy and happiness. I look back now and realize that wasn't my colleague's question. She asked about my *relationship* with joy, not whether I have experienced it.

I've got intimacy, knowledge, and a deep understanding with my own experiences of anger, grief, and fear. They are old friends, and I set a place at the table for them. My comfort with them in others feels familiar and cozy, like I know who I am when I am in this space, and how to be of service. I know what the emotions feel like, what they want, what they feed on, and what settles them down. Like a relationship with a loved one, I travel with them as passengers on my journey.

I realize that I can't say the same for joy and happiness. I welcome them when they are present, rejoice in their visits, and sometimes plan space for the possibility they can be invited to my table. However, we aren't intimate or close friends, and I haven't sought to understand them, cultivate, and nurture them. When you work in the shadows of conflict, quelling controversy, and calming rage, you devote far more energy and time to building capacity to be with those emotions and assume joy and positivity will take care of themselves.

Your Comfort With Your Own Emotion

I often ask participants in my sessions about their discomfort level with their own high emotions, or the high emotions of others. Most people say that it is something they avoid, or something that is hard for them. Interestingly, they often rate their ability to be with their own emotions as easier than being with the emotions of others. It's an interesting nuance, and one I'm not sure is true for me. Instead, I see a direct connection to being able to be with your own emotions, to being able to be with the emotions of others. But then, it seems I'm intentional about working through anger, fear, grief, and anxiety, and less intentional about other emotions. Perhaps, like a mirror I've been building my capacity to be with what surrounds me in my work.

Some Emotions Are Really Hard to Be With

Most people have a difficult time with specific emotions, anger, grief, fear, and anxiety. Some people will do almost anything not to have to be in proximity to an angry, frustrated person. They struggle with how to respond, or how to calm the situation down. This is true in our personal lives, and in our work lives too.

Our societal discomfort with grief is so common that people often respond to grief by saying, *"I'm so sorry,"* as if we are responsible for the sadness of another.

No one is born knowing how to navigate these emotions, and it takes self-awareness, a willingness to be with discomfort, and the courage to stay with the suffering to find the insight.

Like any relationship, what you put your energy on grows and strengthens.

When we interact with each other, there is you, me, and there is also the space around our interaction. So often we put all our emphasis on me or you and neglect what is happening in the space between us, and the space around us.

Social Cohesion is Unravelling

As social animals, we impact each other. These impacts affect how we experience, interpret, and assign meaning to the emotions we experience. I'm coming to realize that decades of work in the space of high emotion, in the space of the 'dark side' of anger, fear, grief, and anxiety has created strong neural pathways in my brain; strong tracks of meaning about who I am in these interactions and how to interact with others when they experience these emotions. Perhaps my tracks related to joy and positivity aren't as deeply worn.

When I think about the years of living in a global pandemic, it feels like the space around me is worn down, tired, exhausted, and burnt out. I'm not alone; so many of my clients, participants, and friends are feeling the weight of the space around us. It's not an anecdotal thing, or just each of us picking up on the energy of each other.

In 2022, the World Economic Forum released its list of the top ten risks facing the world. The fourth most severe risk on a global scale over the next ten years is social cohesion erosion. This risk is the polarization, disconnection, and dehumanization we see in the public arena. It is the massive rise in mental health challenges, the despair, anxiety, fear, and grief gripping the collective.

This is the energy in motion in the space around us, translated from the space inside of us and between us to create a heavy, anxious, fearful energy swirling as a backdrop to all of our interactions.

This is why holding space, standing in the fire, and working with the tension is a core leadership competency.

What if we Embraced the Fullness of Our Emotions?

To face this challenge, imagine if we each embraced the full spectrum of emotions, inviting light as much as dark in these times of challenge?

What if we each cultivated joy and positivity as an antidote to fear, grief, and anger?

What impact might this have on each of us personally, and on those around us?

Emotion is at the very centre and heart of our relationships, experiences, perspectives, and the truth we hold about how the world works.

Emotion escalates or de-escalates conflict.

Emotion is core to every part of the human experience.

When we work with our emotions, we perform better, are more effective, connected, and more capable.

Walk the Talk

I live half-time at our home on Wolfe Island in the Thousand Islands between Canada and the USA. It's a place of transition, an island that holds space between nations. It's a perfect symbol of the energy required to hold space.

I took the dog out for a walk down our rural road on a recent winter morning and ran into a neighbour walking her dogs. The wind was blowing snow all around us, and the chill made our faces sting and our eyes water. I was surprised how happy it made me to see another person in the midst of the isolation of a winter pandemic. I asked her how she was because I know she has experienced some loss and hardship lately. She told me about her challenges, exhaustion, and worries.

Then she asked me how I was.

I was deeply tempted to tell her that I was fine. That is so many people's standard answer when we are asked that question. It is my standard answer, often motivated out of a desire to keep my burdens to myself rather than to place them on someone else. Instead of following my norm, I took a deep breath and said, *"I'm really struggling. I feel the weight of everything from the last two years around me and inside me. I'm finding myself pretty deep in a pit of despair most days. It is what it is, but what it is, is hard."* And I burst into tears, snot running from my nose and my cheeks burning from tears.

My neighbour and I spent far too much time on the road hugging each other and talking that day. My toes and fingers felt frostbitten, and I was chilled to the bone as I finally turned and made my way back home.

When I first turned back towards home, I felt ashamed – who was I to share my load and add to her heavy burden? I should have spent more time helping and supporting her. But as I walked through the blowing snow it occurred to me that actually rather than giving in to feeling bad, what I deeply felt was grateful. Gratitude for her kindness, for sharing, for the moment when we both let each other in, if even just for that time on the road on a snowy day when we were both struggling.

It occurred to me that I want more of that in my world. Not the part about crying in the road, the part about being seen, sharing, connecting, and mutual support. I want more conversations where we find the light in the darkness, even if it is just for a moment.

In *Atlas of the Heart,* Brene Brown affirms that vulnerability requires enormous courage. In an earlier chapter I talked about courage as the catalyst emotion, the one that creates the shift between heavy emotions and lighter, more possible ones. When we use courage to choose lightness in the dark, we find connection and meaning.

There is no shame in the struggle. When we open up and share our suffering, we open the door to connection versus burden.

In choosing lightness in the dark and opening ourselves to what is happening, there are some regular practices that support our journey to integration and wholeness.

Choose the courage to be vulnerable when you need some light in the dark. We all need help and support, and the act of sharing your struggles gives others the gift of helping you, as you help them.

Reflect and Practice – Holding Space

There is no easy, straight forward path to holding space.

It takes effort, energy, and practice to flex your leadership muscles to lead from nothing and hold the space in service of others. We will succeed, and we will also fail and get up and do it again. We are all capable of it. It just takes a commitment to something other than yourself, to creating a positive impact on your world.

- Where are you holding space in your life and work?
- What are you committed to beyond yourself?
- What do you want to create in the world?

- How do you stay in those moments of deep discomfort, committed to surfacing the deepest meaning and finding a way forward together?
- How do you find and connect with the space inside of you?
- What practices support you to be open to what is happening in the space?
- What is happening in the space around you right now? What does it feel, sound, look and taste like? Can you get in the practice of pausing to name and reflect on the space and how it impacts the conversation and dynamics between people and the issues?

Reflect and Practice – Inviting Light into the Darkness

Ask yourself questions to integrate the darkness with the light. When you're felled by despair, grief, fear, or anxiety you can ask yourself:

- What wisdom is there for me here?
- What lesson or insight can this moment give me?
- What else do I have within me that I can lean into or draw on?
- What will sustain me to move through this?
- Whom can I trust or lean into right now?

Set an intention each day to cultivate joy and positivity, to go slow and notice moments of beauty and gratitude around you. I'm noticing when the tomato seeds I planted sprout, and I am taking a few moments to urge them along. I'm saying a prayer to the sun rising and marvelling at the oranges and pinks on the horizon. I'm cozying up with a good book, snuggling with the dog, grateful for unconditional love and companionship. I'm pausing to kiss my husband deeply just because I can. I'm watching a comedy and noticing the pleasure of how laughing fills up my entire spirit.

When you work with groups, ask them to invite joy, positivity, and lightheartedness into their interactions too, by:

- Reading a poem, quote, or invocation at the start of sessions to set the tone for possibility, and to invite in courage, vulnerability, and kindness.
- Asking people to share what they are grateful for when they introduce themselves as a way of normalizing that we all have light along with challenges.
- Conduct exercises in brainstorming the most absurd, worst, out-of-the-box ideas you can come up with related to a serious, or difficult topic. When we do this before we dive into serious discussions on important issues, it lightens the mood, increases lightheartedness, and loosens people's attachment to being right. Plus, it is fun!

When we intentionally welcome what is in the space around us, inside of us and between us, and when we cultivate joy, positivity, and connection we extend our range as leaders. We are more whole and able to welcome what comes and recover from what is difficult too.

CHAPTER 12

How Do You Start the Difficult Conversation?

I have a colleague who is a smart, capable, interesting woman. I've worked with her for more than a decade now, and while I was her teacher and mentor at one point, we are now peers.

A few years ago, our work was taking us in different directions, and I suggested she might want to work with a business coach I had previously worked with, who had helped me get clear on the change I wanted to create in the world. I had motives that I acknowledged; I wanted her success, and I also wanted her to find her own voice. I was struggling with hearing her put things into the world I had written, said, taught, and created and thought if she was grounded in her own vision and values there would be less of this in the space between us.

Surprise! Here Comes Challenge When You Least Expect It

Fast forward a year later, and I was preparing to lead a virtual workshop that I was anticipating would take all my skill. I had prepared myself and was feeling ready and open-hearted for the conversation to come, when I picked up my phone to mindlessly scroll through Facebook for a few minutes before I logged on to open the workshop. Just to name the obvious, this is not a recommended way to prepare for a challenging conversation!

When I opened Facebook, I immediately came across a Facebook Live video in action; my business coach was live interviewing my colleague about her work. My first reaction was excitement. This would be fun to watch, and I could cheer her on from afar as she put her message and work into the world. That excitement very quickly changed to anger and deep, boiling frustration.

Is the Story Yours to Tell?

The business coach asked my colleague to tell a story, referencing one he vaguely recalled about a school bus and protesters showing up at a meeting. You will recall a similar story in Chapter 5, in Part 2, of this book about the Tea Party showing up in school buses to crash a community meeting. Perhaps, since the coach had worked with me for a few years he knew the story well, and because she did similar work thought it was her story to tell. She could easily have corrected him, even noting that she knew the story but indicating she would share another one of her own. She didn't do that.

She proceeded to tell my story as if it was her own. As if she was the person who designed and led the process and was there in that moment. She brought the story to life and the only thing a listener could conclude is that she had this experience, learned from it, and it built her work and practice.

But it wasn't her experience, and the story wasn't hers to tell. It was mine.

Surprise Intensifies Reaction

When I look back, I think it's really good that I had a time limit on how much I could sink into my anger in that moment because I had to put my reaction aside so I could lead another conversation with people who would have their own reactions and emotions, where I needed to bring a loving, calm, generous energy and hold the space for them. That workshop gave me a reprieve and time to process in the back of my mind what I had experienced.

Processing my Feelings to Find the Meaning

When I came back to myself after leading the session, I reached out to my business coach to check in with him first and share my, *"What the fuck was that?"* reaction to the situation. Then I worked through a process for myself that helped me understand what my feelings were pointing me to.

I felt betrayed, full of grief and sadness at the act.

I was full of righteous judgement, mingled with insecurity and fear.

What if people heard the story and thought it was actually her experience?

What if in the hearing of the story they thought she was more credible than me, for work she hadn't even done?

The betrayal was strongest – I had gone through the moment of crisis in that story, having to make a difficult decision when no good choice presented itself, and I'd been in the room in that moment to witness and hold space for the challenges. I'd done the hard soul-searching work to reflect on what this experience could teach me about the practice, and how I could learn and perhaps be a better leader because of it. She hadn't done any of it, and yet she was telling the story as if she had been through all of it.

Once I'd gotten clear on what I was really feeling, and what meaning it was pointing me to in terms of my below the line emotions, I asked myself:

- What else is there here for me?
- What else do I feel about this person, relationship, situation, that might provide me with insight and wisdom?

My years of relationship with my colleague included a number of instances of her presenting herself as if she had experience she hadn't earned, in particular, my experience, words, and insights, although never quite so publicly. But that wasn't all there was in our relationship.

There was learning together, travelling, and working, sharing laughter and fears, creating new solutions to challenging situations.

There was kindness and care.

There were all these other things too that were part of our relationship, not just this one moment of anger and betrayal. There was immense goodness in her, and in our relationship too.

What Now?

So, I asked myself what do I want to do moving forward?

I decided we needed to have a conversation. One where I could share my experience, and I could be open and curious to what was going on for her at that moment. A conversation where we could clear the air, address the challenges, and figure out what might be next for us. We needed a brave, honest conversation.

Reflect and Practice – Start a Brave, Honest Conversation

My friend and colleague, Rick Tamlyn says, *"Your life goes in the direction of the conversations you are having."* If you aren't having the conversations you need to, the absence of talking is also a direction – a direction where nothing gets better or gets resolved. If you are yearning for connection, understanding, or resolution it is likely that others are yearning for that too.

Ask yourself:

- What are the brave, honest conversations you need to step into in your life and work?
- What is stopping you from having these conversations?
- Review the suggestions noted below about how to START a conversation. What will you do and say to initiate the conversation?

How to START the Conversation

Start with three simple questions:

1. **How do you want to show up in the conversation?**
   Your attitude and behavior are going to have an enormous influence on the outcome of the conversation. If you think it is going to be a really difficult conversation, it probably will be. If you believe that whatever happens, something good will come out of talking together, then that will likely be the case. If you choose to show up with compassion, courage, integrity, openness, and a commitment to learn and understand, your attitude will influence the interaction. Make a choice about how you go into the conversation.

2. **What are you hoping to achieve in the conversation?**
   Watch for hidden purposes. You may think you have honourable goals, like educating or sharing information, and then start to notice that your language could be interpreted as critical, blaming or condescending. Watch the assumptions you make about the other person in the conversation. You may feel disrespected, intimidated, or ignored by someone else, but be cautious about assuming this was the other person's intention.

3. **How will you get the conversation started?**
   A deep breath and courage are the first step to starting any tough conversation. If you are struggling for words, think about starting the conversation with an invitation to improve the relationship or solve a problem.

Try these conversation prompts:
- *"I have something I'd like to talk to you about. I'm hoping it will help us work together better."*
- *"I'd like to talk to you about _____, but first I'd like to hear from you."*
- *"I need your help with something. When do you have a few minutes to talk?"*

- *"I think we might see this situation differently. I wonder if we could talk so we understand each other better."*
- *"I'm struggling about how things are working right now. Could we talk about it and figure out something that works for both of us?"*

CHAPTER 13

Embodying Brave and Honest
for Yourself

I use the words 'brave, honest conversations' over and over again. I want to pull apart 'brave' to find its meaning for me, so when I stand in it, I know what it calls forth. I also want to pull apart 'honest', because it impacts our conversations, our perceptions with each other, and our relationship to truth within ourselves.

In *CONSOLATIONS: The Solace, Nourishment, and Underlying Meaning of Everyday Words,* the poet and author David Whyte talks about honesty as being the ultimate experience of powerlessness and humility, of sinking into uncertainty and rawly giving oneself over to the brutal, beautiful truth of something, without guile or ornamentation.

The uncertainty of brutal, beautiful truth resonates with me as the deepest form on honesty.

Looking the Honest Truth in the Face

My mother-in-law died a few years ago. She was eighty-nine, one month shy of ninety, a formidable woman of strongly held opinions, deep intellect, and an indomitable spirit. Until that spirit wasn't indomitable anymore, and she chose to be done with living.

Joan held two doctorate degrees at a time when many women in Canada didn't attend university. She travelled the world, often by herself, married late, and gave birth to my husband in her forties. She was smart, knowledgeable, principled, and serious. She was not warm, nurturing, or motherly; we often joked that my husband was raised by wolves, being first cared for by the nannies and then sent off to boarding school at an early age. Just because she wasn't warm doesn't mean she didn't love. I think she loved deeply but was at a loss for how to express it.

I'm getting off track. My mother-in-law died a few years ago. After being diagnosed with a minor health impairment that she found embarrassing and humiliating, for which she might not qualify to have surgery, she consciously decided she didn't want to live any longer. In her own proud way, she told us all was fine, and when we saw her each week for Sunday dinner, we noticed a decline but did not realize the extent of it.

When we eventually realized how bad it was, she was very far gone. She had decided to stop eating and drinking. Some days she would have a bite or two of something or a sip of water, other days nothing at all. She took to her bed, waiting out the days until they were over, not joining others in the retirement residence for activities or meals due to her shame about her medical condition. When she answered our calls, she said everything was fine and she was just a bit tired.

You Might Not Like What Honesty Reveals

We had to sit down with her, my husband and I, and understand and make sense of her choices.

She was done and was ready to die. She stated it plainly and clearly, without sadness or fear. Her honesty was jarring and scary.

Couldn't we persuade her otherwise?

Couldn't our care for her convince her to stay?

My husband had lost his father the year before, and his mother's choice would mean he was an orphan at forty-eight. No matter how old you are when you lose your parents, you are still a child lost in the woods without guidance and protection for a time after they disappear.

What must it have taken for her to look at the truth of her yearning to die and speak it so clearly?

Did her honesty make it easier or harder for my husband to make choices?

What he wanted -was for her to recover from this setback and continue to live – and what she wanted-which was to finish this life – were incompatible.

There was her honest truth, and my husband's honest truth – and they were different. He had to do the work to find a shared honest truth that honoured both of them.

Honesty as Humility Grounded in Letting Go

He found it within himself to support her wishes, to make choices on her behalf that were what she wanted, rather than what he wanted as she was moved to palliative care and slowly faded away over the next few weeks. Her honesty was pure and clear, and also brutal in its impact.

His honesty was in service, out of love, grounded in grieving.

- How often do we look deeply enough within ourselves to find the truth of what needs to be said?
- How often do we listen deeply enough to hear the honest words of another?
- What might it be like if we frequently met each other in that honest space, with courage and compassion?
- Would we be fully seen in our seeing of others?

What Is Brave?

If honesty is in our seeing of others and in our being seen, then where is courage?

In my experience, living brave in your life, organization, and community needs to be nurtured in ways that are wildly counterintuitive from the idea of armouring up and heading into battle. Stepping into courage is the catalyst that allows us to shift ourselves and others emotionally from below the line to above the line so we can creatively problem solve and deepen understanding.

- **Brave is vulnerability.** It isn't brave unless your messy leaks out. You've got to be fully, really, totally present, and willing to show up in all your beauty and mess. When you do that, you can access your courage, because you are in touch with your emotions. There is no easy path. It takes bravery to be vulnerable.

- **Brave is open-hearted.** Remember the first time you said, *"I love you"*? Remember the time you reached out to a friend or family member at a time in need and said, *"I need help"*? It takes loving, caring, compassion, and empathy to be brave. To risk rejection, failure, and misunderstanding, and still get up and do it again and again.

- **Brave is every day.** Brave isn't a thing you save until there is a really big issue or situation. Brave is how you show up every day with your team, family, community, and for yourself. Brave is where you stretch and grow out of complacency into possibility.

- **Brave is action-oriented.** Overthinking, getting it perfect, and wanting to be certain is paralyzing. Sometimes you have to just do it. Take a risk without all the answers, open your heart to possibility – believe you can do it, and possibility will emerge.

- **Brave is scared, nervous, and afraid, and doing it anyway.** Brave is not fearless. Fearless is a myth. No one is fearless. We are human and so we are all scared, nervous, and fearful at times. Brave is acknowledging, owning, and then feeling the fear – and stepping up and forward anyway.

- **Brave is failure.** The act of believing is far more courageous than waiting until you can see success. The learning is in the trying and not succeeding, and in getting up and beginning again.

- **Brave is commitment.** My colleague, Rick Tamlyn, always asks *"What are you committed to more than your fear?"* How do you want to show up in the world and what impact are you trying to create? You don't need to be brave for everything, but when it's called for it matters that you are committed to it 100percent.

- **Brave is for the really hard stuff and the really beautiful stuff too.** We sometimes forget that beautiful things also require us to be brave. Getting married, giving birth, or welcoming a child into a family, changing jobs, moving to a new city or country, joyfully fulfilling dreams like climbing mountains, saying goodbye to an ill or elderly family member...these beautiful moments are the things that life is made of. To celebrate them, and mark them in our lives, requires us to show up bravely with open hearts so we can be present for every moment of the beauty.

My husband was all these things as he supported, cared for, witnessed, and followed his parents at the end of their lives. Deeply honest, honouring his truth and their truths too. And full of courage, with an open heart, being present for all of it, letting go of what 'should' be, and focusing on what was really important.

Reflect and Practice – Being Brave and Honest

When faced with the hardest conversations of our lives, you need to ask yourself:

- What is this moment calling for from me?
- What do these people need from me?
- How do I tap into and connect with my source of courage?
- How can I hold the uncertainty that comes with total honesty, and be humble enough to witness and acknowledge what is really true here?
- How do I honour my truth, and also the truth of others?
- When I am brave, what does it look and feel like?
- How can I be fully present to the beauty, wonder, and bittersweet moments of the most difficult conversations of my life?

If you can answer those questions with the painful honesty they often require, you can be present and bear witness to the most important moments of your life. Sometimes, the moments feel beautiful, and sometimes they feel as if they are too much to bear. Either way, the seeds of courage and honesty are within you to nurture and grow.

Part 3 takes us on the wild ride that it is to be fully human, open to joy and pain, wonder and frustration, connection and loneliness. We deepen our own self-knowledge when we seek the meaning found in our emotions and build our capacity to hold space for everything that is within us, within others, and in the space around us. When we do this, we lead powerfully, create positive impact, and bring people together. This work is the work of our lives.

PART 4

Leadership in the Systems and Structures Around Us

In Part 4 we recognize there is you, others, and the space of the brave, honest conversation. How we work with all of it is the measure of our leadership in our lives, organizations, and communities.

There is a complexity in this space where the structures we work with, and the systems we are part of collide in incongruent ways with the conflicts we experience.

We need to look for patterns, insights, and growth at the edges of our experiences in order to transform from what was to what is emerging. When we step fully into new skills, knowledge, and ways of being as a leader, we contribute to a world where the divide between people narrows, where connection, trust, and relationships grow, and where together we solve the problems we face.

CHAPTER 14

From Polarization to Possibility

When we break down highly polarized issues into their respective parts, a different picture can emerge. We can go from against each other, to for each other, but the journey isn't simple or easy.

Breaking Down a Highly Polarized Issue

In 1992, Canadian Blood Services introduced a lifetime ban on blood donation by any man who has had sex with another man. Viewed through today's moral lens, it was a homophobic policy based in fear and born out of a scandal related to tainted blood, where one segment of the population was targeted.

In the early 2000's, the organization was taken to court, claiming the policy was a human rights violation. In 2010 the Ontario Superior Court ruled that the blood ban was not a human rights violation, due to safety issues. In essence, it wasn't a human right to donate blood.

In 2013, Canadian Blood Services reduced the ban on blood donation from a lifetime restriction to five years; a man could donate blood if he had not had sex with another man in the last five years.

In 2016, Canadian Blood Services reduced the ban from five years to one year, in 2019 the blood donation ban was reduced from one year to three months, and in 2022 at the time of writing, there are indications it may be removed completely.

Over the course of twenty years the policy went from claims of a human rights violation to being shelved. That change required deliberation, dialogue, and a major shift in thinking.

There Is Always a Human, Emotional Side to Every Polarized Situation

The dates documenting policy change don't give us a window into the heart-wrenching, heated conversations that resulted in this progress, and the countless hours of raised voices that created change. There were real human beings caught in the middle of this policy:

- Patients and blood recipient groups literally afraid for their lives if anything should taint the blood supply.
- People who were angry, frustrated, and in despair about the unfairness of a system that treated them as second-class citizens, not good enough to make a contribution to others by virtue of their sexuality rather than the scientific evidence.
- Staff, researchers, and scientists at the agency who wanted to get things right, afraid of making the wrong choice, and the consequences of that choice for anyone involved, struggling with changing norms and a lack of scientific evidence that could clearly point the way forward.

When What You Are Doing Isn't Working, You Need to Try Something New

Can you picture an evidence and science-based organization struggling with the loss of public trust, negative perception, and changing social norms over almost twenty years to make significant shifts in public policy?

The leadership required to step into the fire of the public arena, in the midst of chaos and turmoil, to learn, listen, and respond in different ways was immense.

Let's step back to some of the actions that resulted in these seismic shifts.

In 2012, I was hired by Canadian Blood Services to plan, facilitate, and report on a series of conversations about the blood donation policy for men who have sex with other men. The conversations came on the heels of years of blockades, protests, and advocacy campaigns with the slogan, 'All blood is equal,' and happened after being taken to court with claims of human rights violations.

Canadians had stopped donating blood in required amounts, and the blood supply was declining.

The organization was perceived as unresponsive, homophobic, and unfair by many in the public arena, and public sentiment was stacked against them. They had significant negative public perception challenges on their hands.

What was happening inside the organization was a culture of fear, risk aversion, and a feeling of being under siege. For many who worked there, it had gone from a place of work with purpose and meaning to a place of uncertainty, embarrassment, and stigma.

Planning to Talk About Hard Things in the Middle of a Storm

When the agency reached out to me to help them with conversations on this controversial issue, I was curious and also hesitant. Who did they want to talk to? What was their goal? What would happen with the results of the conversation? I asked a lot of questions as we began to plan, and I urged them to rethink some of their original ideas.

Initially, the organization wanted to engage only stakeholders of groups who rely on blood donations; groups like the Hemophilia Society, Heart & Stroke Foundation, Kidney Foundation among others, and ask them what they were prepared to agree to before entering into a conversation with members of the community groups. Their thinking was that those who received blood should hold a 'trump card' for any changes that might potentially emerge related to the lifetime ban for men-who-have-had-sex-with-other-men blood donation policy.

I cautioned them against this approach, noting that if one group has a veto, then the conversation isn't equitable, fair, open, inclusive, or transparent – it doesn't meet any test of meaningful engagement.

If you are going to ask people what they think, and have separate conversations with polarized groups where they can't hear or understand each other's answers, and then give one side all the power, there really isn't any point bringing groups together to have a conversation.

If that is the plan, it is probably best to just decide on the course of action you want to take and move forward, informing everyone of your choice.

Do Things Differently

It is a testament to the organization's desire to get this deeply polarizing, emotional issue right that they were humble enough to rethink their initial approach. They asked me what I would recommend, and I suggested that they:

- Bring together or solicit the most recent research and a cross section of experts in the field to make sure the conversation was grounded in all available evidence, research, and information about blood borne illnesses
- Reach out to both 'sides' and ask them to identify participants for a conversation where everyone would come together to understand the facts, deliberate on choices, trade-offs, and consequences, and potentially map out a path forward.
- At the same time, launch a concurrent public conversation about the polarized issue to raise awareness and understanding of the complexity of changes to the policy, and invite Canadians into a series of in person and online conversations to talk together.

It was an ambitious plan, grounded in the organization presenting a face that was humble, transparent, and stepping right into the midst of the controversy, with a faith that people would find a way to close the divide as they connected and deepened understanding. It was an approach that would generate solutions built on deep understanding and deliberation.

The organization said thanks, but that the approach was too much, too big, and too uncomfortable for them. They came back with a modified approach:

- Bring together or solicit the most recent research, and a cross section of experts in the field to make sure the conversation was grounded in all available evidence, research and information about blood borne illness.
- Reach out to both 'sides' and ask them to identify participants for a conversation where each side would come together *separately* to understand the facts, deliberate on choices, trade-offs, and consequences. That would mean blood donor and recipient groups would talk with each other, and LGBTQ2S+ groups would talk with each other, but the two 'sides' wouldn't come together to connect or learn from each other. Then the agency would review the input of each side and propose a way forward.
- There would be no public wide conversation to engage in a national discussion on the policy, but a public opinion poll would be run to gauge where Canadians stand on the issue.

It took courage to step into the unknown of these conversations, to explore with stakeholders their experiences, perspectives, and needs. It took courage for stakeholders to be in the conversation, willing to talk about their fears and concerns, and committed to finding a way forward.

Brave, Honest Conversations About Complex Issues Are Bound to Be Messy

Blame is easy. Polarization can feel familiar, picking a side of good and bad, and putting yourself on the side of angels. It can make you feel good and superior, better than those on the other side.

The opinions on each side can feel righteous and certain, but they don't create the space for forgiveness, accountability, healing, and finding a way forward. They are just opinions that inflame the space around the conflict.

Opinions are like votes on an issue, and are about aligning ourselves with a side, a side righteously defined as right or wrong. Votes and opinions are about winning, not about de-escalating the conflict.

When we clearly define the sides in a conflict as right or wrong, or good and bad, things will escalate. Sides are like the childhood game of red rover where children line up across a great divide, holding hands tightly. Then they call someone from the other side over, but their goal isn't to have them join their line; instead, it is to create a wall they can't break through. People get injured running into the line, feelings are hurt, and eventually, one side 'wins,' and the other side loses. It was one of my least favourite childhood games and remains a great analogy for the divide of conflict and the rise of toxic polarization.

Many of us are lucky to live in societies where we have a right to raise our voice and express our opinions. However, it is not enough to have a right. A right on its own lacks integrity without responsibility. We live in societies where right is paramount—the right to protest, march, petition, disengage, blame, shame, and ridicule, the right to attack, discriminate, and slander – online and in person.

We've created an illusion that when we sign a petition, post on Facebook, or march in a protest that we've changed the world. Often, we haven't changed much—we've contributed to the collective exhale of opinions, opposition, or resistance, without creating the future we are calling for. We haven't seen into the hearts of those who see the world differently than we do, or who hold different opinions. Usually, we've talked to people who believe what we do, and demonized and separated ourselves from others, often justifying that they are wrong, and we are right.

When we value right over responsibility, we are all for one, and no one for all. We value our own right to an opinion over the needs of our neighbours, those who are marginalized, or the collective good.

We need to bring back responsibility—for the quality of our democracy, for the practice of talking with each other, for the ability to truly solve tough challenges in our lives, organizations, and communities.

There is your truth, my truth, and the divide between us. The space between us; that's where we resolve conflict.

In the first conversations about the blood donation policy, participants on each side asked when they could talk to people on the other side. While the agency had kept them apart out of fear and a desire to protect each side from a potentially harsh and hurtful conversation, over and over again they asked for each other. They wanted to know how the other side would answer the question they had just answered, they were curious about the experiences and perspectives that were different from their own. They were yearning for deeper understanding of each other – a precursor to a shift in the conflict. They recognized that this conflict needed both sides to find a way forward.

What created that shift in experience and perspective?
What created the yearning to be with others who see the situation differently than you do?

Conflict Feeds on Simplicity; Complexity Supports Conflict Transformation

When we try to define sides as right or wrong, good or bad, we are attempting to simplify a situation and also to identify others who think the same as we do. Those acts further inflame conflict because it is rarely simple or easy to solve.

When we introduce complexity, we require people to grapple with the patterns and nuances of a situation, and to more deeply understand and work to find a new way forward that looks at the whole picture, rather than the parts of the whole. In this situation, both sides had to grapple with the available evidence, research, and science, as well as the conflict playing out in the public arena. It might be safe and comfortable to stay in the bubble of their side, but they were stuck there.

What can be difficult is holding the space in the middle, being in the mess and division, and looking for a way forward together. When we make the other side wrong, and then we dehumanize them, we've lost our own humanity in the process. When we find ourselves in this space, we can ask ourselves and the others who are there with us the following questions:

- What is the anger, fear and despair pointing me to? What is the lesson or teaching for me to find there?

- If I can enter into the anger and name its source, can I find liberation and freedom there? Can I channel enough love and compassion to understand the lessons anger or fear wants to teach me?

- In this tumultuous, chaotic time, what does the world need more of? What can I contribute?

- Who is it that I need at my back? Whose back do I need to have? Who do I need to connect with, to step aside for, or hold space for so we could find a way forward?

- How do I find the strength and resilience to work in the discomfort, to do hard things together with others?

I know that conversation is the conduit to connection, understanding, relationships, and trust. When those things are present, we can accomplish anything, together. In a world of polarization there is little or no connection, understanding, relationship, or trust. What the participants in this first conversation about the blood donation policy began to experience and learn, is that when they were in the trench with each other, their own understanding deepened, and they could see the needs of others and allow their own needs, fear, and anger to be seen and acknowledged as well.

Open Your Heart and Others Will Follow

When we lead difficult polarized conversations, we need to model the dynamic we are asking people to embody. If I remember that we are for each other's hopes, needs, and differences, then I can hold space to celebrate those differences, and to foster understanding so we can be in it together.

If I lead with my heart, I show up fully in the hardest moments. Even when our hearts break over the state of tragedy, trauma, chaos, and disconnection in the world, our hearts can break open instead of into pieces. That breaking open can allow us to hold the complexities and compassion of being fully human together.

In that space we can find solutions to impossible situations.

In crisis and challenge, we sink or swim, and our real spirit shows through. In times of chaos, disruption, and turmoil, we can choose to be part of the solution, to offer compassion, possibility, and courage to what is to come. We can believe that we can do hard things together. Once we believe that, we dig into the conversation, committed to each other and the possibility we can find solutions together.

There Are No Top Ten Tips That Transform Conflict

I have a personal button that gets pushed when people offer their top ten tips, or three easy techniques to resolve conflict. These simple tips discredit the deep complexity that comes with polarized conflict and encourages us to think that if we just do this one thing, then everything will be better. It creates false expectations and contributes to transactional approaches that often result in dehumanization, manipulation, or disrespect in our high stakes interactions with each other.

You need skills, knowledge, and ways of being to transform conflict, and the solution is often as complex as the conflict itself.

We need to see the immediate event, and then see the patterns that form the context for this conflict, and then we need to hold the issues and the ways of thinking and being that all contribute to transforming the conflict at the same time.

In every conflict, there is you, me, and the space of the conflict.

In the conflict at Canadian Blood Services, there is the side of patients and blood recipients advocating for a safe blood supply, and there is the side of LGBTQ2S+ groups advocating for fairness and human rights; and there is the agency, seeking to find a fair AND safe blood system.

(Just a note that at the time of writing the acronym LGBTQ2S+ was commonly used as an inclusive way of acknowledging different people. Terms and language are constantly evolving and if the language has changed since this was written, we hope you read this knowing our commitment is to inclusion.)

Then there is EVERYONE ELSE in the space. Over many years, the space was so loud that its energy was expanding as the conflict was escalating, with clear sides being defined. This is where media coverage, social media amplification, marches, protests, petitions, and blockades emerged.

In the space of this conflict, it is important to note that no one can transform a conflict by themselves. Changing the space of the conflict requires a new approach that works with the complexity of the issue, takes multiple paths at the same time, and involves multiple people within the system. We must learn together, deliberate together, question assumptions, and seek new ways of thinking together, and through it all connect at a human level – together.

Focus on Alignment Versus Agreement

When I am asked to guide people out of conflict into something new and different, I always begin by talking about emotion as a path to making meaning, establishing relationships, and developing trust and centering shared humanity.

Start With the People Not the Issues

Once we see each other as fully human, we can begin the slow process of talking about the issues. I don't start with the issues – we already know we don't agree on them.

Instead, let's be fully, messily, beautifully human together in all of our differences and similarities and let's celebrate that humanity. When I can really see you as a flawed and gorgeous person with your own loves, values, and hopes, and you can see me that way, then we can begin to talk.

It's a Myth You Don't Have Time to Center People in the Conversation

Sometimes, people suggest we don't have time to do this, or that it's unprofessional to talk about our feelings. Instead, it's time we agree that feelings matter. They aren't the only things that matter but they are more important than we think. They are part of being fully human, required for fulsome and sustainable decision-making, and a reality of having brave, honest conversations. The sooner we release the myth that we are a rational, fact-based society governed solely by science and data, the sooner we can move on to solving real problems.

It matters that we put heart at the centre of our tough conversations. Caring is the key to building trust and strengthening relationships. It is not a coincidence that trust in public institutions has declined as we have increased our reliance on facts over feelings. When we have a conflict or public opposition on an issue, we can't separate the issue from the people.

Facts don't make people feel better, but feelings allow people to be seen and validated, so they can talk about the facts.

Cancel Culture Cancels the Humanity in All of Us

As part of centering humanity, we need to remember that we are all flawed, and mistakes are core to growth and learning. No one is defined by a single action or behaviour. In a society that is volatile and polarized, the public arena goes quickly to blame and shame, condemning people by a single act rather than the fullness of who they are.

The conflict about the blood donation policy – and so many other conflicts – result in the dehumanization of each side. In this case one side was characterized as homophobic and discriminatory, and the other side was characterized as uncaring, unsafe, and taking risks with people's lives. When we go to these extremes, we lose the nuances of the complete human who may have uttered a sentence out of fear or anger, and we define them by one act, one statement, one situation. We cancel them, which is an act of total disregard for another human.

I started this book with a story about me being the target of public shaming online. This phenomenon is over in a moment for many who lash out online but has lasting personal and professional impacts on those who are attacked. There are human costs to this way of interacting.

The author Maya Angelou once said, "*When someone shows you who they are, believe them.*" This is about our own perceptions, and that when someone demonstrates to us who they are, believe that, rather than relying on who they say they are. We need to go beyond surface level when we apply this wisdom – there are the fears, anger, and indignation that are expressed, and also so very much more that tell us about the fullness of the stories and lives lived by these human beings.

In order to transform conflict, we must resist the urge to dehumanize others by defining them by a single act or action.

Conflict Transformation Requires Changes in Me, in You, and in the System

Take the time to find out what threatens the other person and then stop doing it, taking full responsibility for the impact of your choices.

In every conflict, it is important to look for opportunities for accountability, responsibility for impact, and rebuilding trust. Choose how you show up and what your intentions are in de-escalating the conflict. Consider the impact of your actions, thoughts, and behaviours, and take responsibility. Make conciliatory gestures and offer to create lasting change.

It matters that you believe in the possibility of a brave, honest conversation and have faith in what can happen when people come together to talk with each other about tough issues.

- When you come from a place of unconditional, positive regard you manifest that in others and in the conversation.
- When you commit to working through the conflict and to finding solutions, that commitment echoes when things get heated.
- When you are open to possibility, to new ideas, to deeply understanding other ways of thinking and seeing the world, you hold space for transformation to emerge.
- When you practice empathy and commit to building trust and relationships, others follow suit.

- When you know what you stand for, why you are showing up as a leader, participant, or facilitator, when you consciously choose 'yes' to finding new solutions and deeply commit to inclusion, trust, responsibility, and the important conversations we need to have, you can change the world.

It is about more than what you do or what you know, it is about how you want to be. To do that, first, you need to choose where you stand, and what you stand for.

The court case, blockades, and protests in this situation were much more than demonstrations. They were an opportunity to make systemic change in a system that wasn't serving everyone. They were an opportunity to centre humanity and move away from blame, shame, and toxic polarization. They were an opportunity for each of us to take responsibility for voicing our opinions and contributing to positive change, or to raise our voices in the clamour of being right and growing the divide between people.

Reflect and Practice – Increase Complexity

In order to transform conflict, you need to increase complexity within yourself, for others, and within the conversation. When you change patterns of thinking and feeling, making different choices in your interactions, you can find more effective ways to transform conflict. Here are some ways to increase complexity in your next polarized conflict:

Choose to soften versus cling to rigidity – When you are certain about your view, you are blind to the fact that you have said, done, or thought things that contradict the simple view you are holding right now. When you use words like 'never' and 'always', when we find ourselves judging others harshly – these are good indicators that your views have gotten rigid. Soften your thinking and remember that within you there are many different perspectives and feelings.

Intentionally connect with difference – Practice curiosity and inquiry about the situation or topic. Intentionally explore views different from your own. Reach out to others who have expressed alternate viewpoints and ask genuine questions, seeking to understand their story and experience. Expose yourself to alternate media and world views.

Flip perspectives –Ask yourself and others flip questions to choose a wider, broader view of the conflict. For example:

- What would someone who describes this issue differently from you want us to know or understand?
- If I was a _____ (different gender, race, religion, political affiliation etc. than you align with) how would I see this situation?
- What might I be blind to? What might I not be seeing or understanding here?

Increase cognitive complexity–What are all the different facts, perspectives, ideas, dynamics, experiences, and nuances that make up this issue? What is the real problem? When you expand your understanding of the topic, you expand your understanding of how challenging it might be to solve. What is most important to different people about this issue, and how do they see it? What are the consequences or choices that will impact what happens here? Consider the situation from all sides before coming to any conclusion.

CHAPTER 15

Leading With Love

I'm working with two other leaders I have the deepest respect and admiration for, who walk the talk of leadership in difficult situations. Together, we've collaboratively designed a leadership program to build capacity to create positive change in a world of complexity, disruption, and chaos. It has taken every bit of knowledge, skill, and being I've got to build this program. It stretches me every day, growing it and making it better, and learning from what works and what doesn't.

Know Your Role Before You Lead

On this day, we are leading a virtual workshop 'Indigeneity and leadership in a colonial structure,' with thirty participants of indigenous descent in the far north of Canada. Two of us are settler allies and one is of indigenous descent.

We need to play dramatic and clear roles in this session, distinguishing between who holds story and lived experience, who has knowledge and skill related to leadership content, and who is holding the space for difficult conversations.

Know What You Are Committed To

Before we begin, we need to unpack our own hopes and fears for the session, uncovering the worries and perceptions we want to avoid. I want to stand clearly in my commitment to convene and hold space for people to talk about the most difficult things. I want to honour stories of racism, discrimination, tokenism, and lived experience I know will emerge without emotionally reacting to the extent that my empathy overtakes my ability to be in service.

My colleague, who has served as a First Nation Chief, doesn't want to be perceived as trying to speak for all indigenous people. She wants to speak her truth, not everyone's truth, and bring her unique experience, insights, and perspective to the table.

My other colleague wants to be seen as an ally, and to watch that her own discomfort with talking about hard things doesn't create discomfort for participants, and to guide and support them to grow the authentic leadership that connects identity, culture, and values.

Bring Your Whole Self and Take Responsibility for Impact

It's a delicate line for each of us to walk as we lead these workshops – bringing our whole self to leadership AND taking responsibility for impact. Authenticity is so often seen as a license to "*let it all hang out,*" and "*you do you*" as my children would say. Instead, authenticity is more closely connected to a grounding in your identity, strengths, and values, and living from that place.

When we authentically lead, we need to dance with being ourselves, and also take responsibility for the impact of our choices, actions, and words.

Finding Yourself Hooked by Wanting to Be Right

It's human nature that we live our lives in search of certainty, to confirm whatever we think or believe is 'right', and that others are 'wrong'. It's a pendulum that swings from side to side, and in recent years the space of all of our interactions have become more reactive, more focused on 'likes' and 'friends', the implication being that there are 'others' who we don't like and who aren't our friends. We live in a time of outrage, a time that has exacerbated our human nature to pick sides, pick groups, and cement our opinions as if they are truth.

Even when you know this and work with it every day, you can find yourself living out the pendulum swing in order to be certain and right.

Together with these two colleagues that I dearly love working with, we were interviewed for a podcast by another brilliant, and talented colleague. We were asked *"What are the skills and ways of being that are most needed by leaders to lead at this time, to navigate this time of chaos and disruption, and move us forward?"* It is a big juicy question, and one that I hope this book provides some answers to.

My first colleague answered and talked about collaboration and working with diversity well to get better results by honouring different experiences and worldviews. She talked about bringing voices forward with humility and listening from the heart. She noted how collaboration, compassion, and vision are all needed to address systemic, long-standing challenges, noting that the pandemic has created opportunities to really see and talk about the big issues we are facing.

When my second colleague responded, I could begin to feel myself sliding into a side of the right/wrong pendulum, my physical reaction rising like heat in my chest, wanting to challenge or correct her, wanting to be right (and make her wrong).

She talked about needing to find common ground, harmony, and sameness so people can be connected to each other. She referenced the need to go slow and carefully, and to listen deeply. She talked about calming the nervous system and finding safety and harmony between people. She talked about the need to be able to be with difference, to put our egos in the back seat, to let go of the past or things we were certain of.

Reckoning With Sameness and Difference

On the surface what she said all sounds like something I can't disagree with, and yet there are tensions in her words with what my twenty-five plus years in conflict transformation has taught me. I felt affronted, confronted, and made wrong. When I look to how I have come to this moment, consider the family I grew up in where harmony and sameness were prized and conflict was avoided and made wrong. When I heard my friend emphasize harmony, I interpreted she was making all that I stood for and believed in wrong. I interpreted that she was saying harmony is better than difference. These are my stories and interpretations, my reactions to her words.

I know that sameness is the source of familiarity and comfort…but it is a dry well for innovation and solving complex problems.

I know that a little conflict is a rich fertilizer for thinking in new and different ways, for seeing old problems with new eyes, and for deepening understanding.

I know that listening well is crucial, and sometimes slowing down means people cling to getting it 'right' or perfect, and chaos and disruption requires us to try, fail, iterate, learn, and get up and do it again until something sticks or works.

I know that safety is important to surface honest tensions and differences…and too much harmony and safety can stifle that very divergence of perspective that we seek for conflict transformation.

Can You Hold Two Competing Truths at One Time?

So, what did I do? Is it possible to hold two competing truths at the same time? Can I make her right and also share my truth? I'd love this to be a story about how once you build a skill or knowledge, you always have it, and can access it when you need to. Instead, the reality is that on this day I did some of what was needed, stepping into my better self, and I also held onto my ego.

Here is my response to the big juicy question on the podcast about the leadership the world needs now, and the irony is not lost on me that what I am calling for in the world is what I was calling for from myself in that moment. Isn't that when awareness can become wisdom? When we dip deeply into our own frailties and strengths and turn them towards the world in service to something greater than ourselves? It's often messy, and sometimes it's impactful.

Discomfort as a Source of Change

"I will build on what my colleagues have said. We need leaders who can stand in the fire. Sometimes it's easy to think, let's define the problem, let's have a conversation, let's gather the right people...that's a start. I think staying is much harder than starting. Especially when we are looking at complex problems and a wild divide between people. So, staying is a leadership requirement, even if it's not a skill. That is about building our comfort with discomfort. Not just our awareness of it.

Can I change my perception of it, and can I stay with the real thing that is rising, now that the heart of things are coming out? Now we see the source of this challenge. Instead of seeing this discomfort as a thing we always need to smooth, we can see that there is beauty in the discomfort. While there is beauty in harmony there isn't a lot of innovation in harmony, and at the moment what we need is a lot of innovation. We need differences to solve the challenges we are facing. It is crucially important that we shine a light on the challenges and the divide – like systemic racism, inequities, complex challenges. The work of leaders is not in calling out the challenges, because that is kind of easy, pointing out what is wrong, what doesn't work, that these are the folks who created the bad system...that doesn't result in any change. It furthers the divide a little further.

Instead, leaders do their best work when they call it in, welcome it in, welcome in the thing we've shone the light on, and welcome everyone into the conversation because when we move forward all together, then we have an opportunity to solve the challenges. If we leave folks behind, at the sides of the road, or leave half the people who are on the other side behind, then we haven't solved anything, we've just switched sides. Then who didn't have the power before will have it now, and everyone else will be left behind. Those are really hard competencies to get people to embody.

It's much harder to stand in the discomfort and shift your perception and welcome it and see it as an opportunity. It's much more difficult to welcome in people who you think have abhorrent views, or who you flat out disagree with, and ask them to be part of solving the problem with you and be part of making change. There are no band-aids to the leadership the world needs now. It requires this dance of doing things and also showing up, there is this dance of doing and being. Courage is often there when we take a breath and step into it, and we need compassion too, so we can hold the space for everyone."

Shared Truth

I believe every word I said, and I know from deep experience that in my bones it is true. And I also know that there is more than one truth. My colleague's call for harmony, interdependence, and connection is also truth. We can't stand in courage and discomfort all the time, or we will lose our resilience. My colleague's assertion that we need to slow things down and be reflective and cautious is also true. The energy it takes to try, fail, iterate, and dig deep means we will need to step back. We need to see the patterns and wisdom in the web of tension that are emerging, and we can only do that in stillness.

I'm not right and she's not wrong. Together, we create the parts of the whole that are needed in these times.

And one more thing. When I am totally honest with myself, I also can feel the blister from the rub where I answered the question from a place with a tiny seed of frustration, competition, and ego. I mostly tapped into an open-heart to answer the question, but the little rub of wanting to be right ran deep, and it was still there. I was sending messages about being right, even as I acknowledged we are both right, even if I think I might be a little more right! When we really look into it, the universe is never an either/or, yes/no, right/wrong equation. The universe is always patterning integration for us. We are all these things and so much more.

For example, I am open-hearted and also want to be right. We need to stand in the fire of discomfort, and also seek stillness and the familiarity and comfort of sameness.

Things only fall apart, and rifts only widen when we try to make the complex simple, as if there really is a right side and a wrong side. As an elder once said to me, *"A bird has a left wing and a right wing, and it needs both to fly."* The sides in this time of outrage have been manufactured by humans in an attempt to bring us comfort in chaos and disruption, yet instead have brought us divide and disconnection.

Love and Leadership

Our antidote is in courage and compassion and holding multiple truths at once. We need to recognize when we've grounded ourselves in that, and when we haven't, and also when we need to get up and dust ourselves off and try again another day.

In an interview for '*On Being*,' Black Lives Matter co-founder, Patrisse Cullors,, talked about how love has been suffused in their activism. "*It's both rage and love at the center of our work*," she says. "*When we show up on the freeway, when we chain ourselves to each other, that's an act of love. That act of resistance is an act of love, that we will put our bodies on the line for our community and for this country. In changing black lives, we change all lives.*"

The antidote to fear, polarization, and the divide between us is human kindness. Let's bring that word LOVE into our workspaces, our communities, our conversations with strangers, and new connections. If outrage has been normalized, perhaps we can normalize love as another choice.

There appears to be a link between leadership and love. I stumbled across a video by Dr. Joe Ricciardi, a Lt. Colonel in the U.S. Army Reserves (see https://youtu.be/nV8_0kt2VVg).

Dr. Ricciardi explored the intersection between love and leadership in his dissertation for the Centre for Values-Driven Leadership. The essence of his thesis is that if you want to be successful you need to love one another. He states in the video: "*Intimacy, passion, and commitment are core elements of love. There is a significant positive relationship between love and leadership. Those leaders that display intimacy, passion, and commitment to those they lead are seen as better leaders. Intimacy is the component that shines through.*" (Used by permission.) In a world struggling with a growing divide this is much needed and inspiring research.

We've been socialized to think that talking about love, compassion, and empathy in a work setting or the public arena is inappropriate or taboo. We have been taught that love is a thing to be kept hidden, in private, just between you and me.

Our norms tell us that love doesn't exist at work, in our neighbourhoods or communities, or for strangers in the public arena. There is this sense that if we talk about love at work or with people who aren't members of our family that we are weak and soft, maybe even silly.

It is time we challenged that idea.

Why does it make us uncomfortable to talk about LOVE in a work setting or the public arena? I recently led a workshop with people working in not-for-profit organizations who are working on the ground to find and implement solutions to complex challenges like: the opioid epidemic, discrimination based on gender and sexual identity, poverty, and reconciliation.

These people are doing hard work at the grassroots level, tackling complex challenges with limited funding or resources. In our session, the word love came up when we talked about leadership. A workshop participant offered it hesitantly and with discomfort at first. We were talking about what really needs to be present in order to have a brave, honest conversation, and how you need to be in order to lead these challenging discussions. Her group had been deep in discussion about brave, honest conversations and identified these factors:

- Good intentions alone are not enough. There also needs to be action and attention to the impact of your actions.
- Consider everyone's needs equally.
- Disrupt gender socialization.
- Hold space in your mind for the possibility that the conversation might be fun, uplifting and affirming, and not just hard and grueling.
- Take accountability for your role and impact.
- Be ready to be present and listen deeply; and
- **Lean into love.**

Lean into Love

When you think about those most difficult of conversations and the leadership it requires to step into them, why wouldn't you choose love and compassion over expertise, being right, or certainty? If we can talk together about our sources and perspectives on hate, fear, grief, and anxiety, then why can't we talk about love?

If you give people a choice between fear and the status quo they will lean into fear, because humans are hardwired from an evolutionary perspective to watch out for danger and protect themselves and what matters most.

Fear closes us down, isolates us, and makes us protective. In the last few years (and over the course of history) we have seen some politicians intentionally generating fear, using it to catalyze action for their causes, and to divide and separate people. Historically, fear of the other has resulted in discrimination, war, and genocide.

However, if you give people a choice between love and fear, they will choose love.

Love is a more powerful force than fear. It generates hope, possibility, creativity, innovation, and problem solving. It connects us to each other and generates positive energy. It opens us up. Love has inspired religions, social movements, and major social changes.

While fear gives people something to be against, love gives people something to be for.

Fear closes us off, isolates us, generates disconnection and separateness. Fear feeds into thinking that 'the other' (those who are different from you) are dangerous, and you need to protect yourselves from them. Fear creates group thinking, gated communities, stagnant organizations, and polarized societies. Why wouldn't you choose love instead?

There is something transformative that happens when we tell our stories and are seen, heard, and acknowledged. Something transformative happens when we have the hardest conversations of our lives.

"Being heard is so close to being loved that for the average person they are almost indistinguishable."

~David Augsburger

This quote echoes in my head when I lead really hard conversations. How do we lead in ways that result in people walking away feeling loved? They don't have to agree, but they should feel valued, worthy, and like they matter. Isn't that the essence of human connection? Can we create those spaces of deep connection, regardless of whether we agree or not?

In my years in the trenches of the public arena, navigating these most challenging of conversations, I have witnessed what doesn't work to bring people together and solve problems. I have also witnessed what does work. It seems to come down to seven core leadership characteristics that are demonstrated time and again when the stakes are high, when a shift is needed, when folks are stuck and dug in, and where it seems nothing will change, until suddenly everything transforms.

Seven Leadership Characteristics the World Needs Now

The seven characteristics of leadership the world needs now are:

- **Authenticity** – Standing fully in your own unique strengths, values, and commitments, in service to what you want to create or bring into the world. Not cloaking yourself in a role, hierarchy, or position, but instead being the full, whole human being you are in this moment, drawing on what this moment and people need from you.

- **Commitment** – Clarity of purpose and vision, grounded in values, oriented towards having a positive impact.

- **Courage** – Working with and stepping into fear, discomfort, chaos, and uncertainty to create a shift, change, or movement to something better.

- **Integrity** – Words, actions, and behaviours all aligned so that your choices are in alignment with your values, and your decisions are transparent, clear, and open.

- **Hope** – Holding a positive orientation to possibility, focusing on what you want more of rather than what you are against, inspiring and encouraging others to move towards building a more positive future.

- **Humility** – Acknowledging and acting from a place that recognizes you don't have all the answers, that you will fail and make mistakes, that your work in the world is better when it is responsive to the needs and views of those around you.

- **Compassion, empathy, and love** – Coming from a place of kindness and care for the humanity in all of us, embracing the messiness of being fully human as a beautiful part of the journey of life.

All seven leadership characteristics are needed. Where you are strong -lean into the attribute. Where you have a growing edge, raise your awareness and work to embody what the moment, people, and situation requires from you.

Reflect and Practice – Leadership the World Needs Now

- Look around to find leaders you admire or who inspire you. What characteristics do they embody? What do these characteristics look like in action in others?
- Consider your own strengths. Which of these seven leadership characteristics are strong in you? How can you lean into them when the moment calls for you to lead? Of these seven leadership characteristics, which of them do you consistently and fully embody?
- Of these seven leadership characteristics, which of them present an opportunity for you to stretch, grow, and improve? Which of these characteristics represent a growing edge for you, that you may need to stretch into? What would it look like for you to grow in these areas? What are some actions you could take? What mindset would support your growth?
- What might it look like to more fully lean into the parts of yourself that are connected to these characteristics, and lead from there? What impact might it have?
- What are some choices you could make to lead more frequently from these seven leadership characteristics?

CHAPTER 16

What Is Really Going on Here?

I'm having déjà vu. I feel like I've been in this house before, listening to this story, sitting drinking yerba mate tea with these people, listening to birdsong out the window. When the alternate memory releases me, I've gapped out, not paying attention to what is happening and need to pull myself back to attention.

The Deepest Beauty of Human Experience

Maria (not her real name) is boiling more water on her wood stove, the walls of her one room house dark with soot from the wood ash. She has offered us her best seats; a worn blue velvet sofa and two chairs at a pine table that has seen countless family meals.

She has no electricity, no running water, but her large greenhouse provides a bounty of vegetables most of the year. Her skin is brown and wrinkled, and her eyes crease at the corners as she smiles with pleasure to have guests from so far away at her table to listen to her story.

She lives here alone; two of her children and her husband are buried in the earth beyond the greenhouse, and her other children scattered to towns and cities around the country to find work.

She looks like she is in her seventies, but I'm told she is fifty-one. The wear of a difficult life shows on her face and body.

We are in a tiny hamlet, a cluster of three homes at the edge of a bright blue glacier fed river, seven hours drive from the nearest city down a long one-lane gravel road called the Great Southern Highway into the wilds of Chilean Patagonia.

I don't speak Spanish, and we have an interpreter, and someone from the area who knows Maria to connect us to her.

I've been brought here to assess the conflict and if possible, find a way forward. A multinational conglomerate has proposed five hydro-electric dams for this remote part of Patagonia, in a UNESCO world heritage site. The proposed project has spawned an international resistance campaign to stop the development. I know what Greenpeace and Save Our Rivers have to say about the project; I want to know what people like Maria think about it.

A Life's Journey Has Richness and Beauty to It

We settle in and listen to her softly musical voice tell her story, with pauses for the interpreter to make sure we understand the words. I'm watching her body, and her face as she speaks, and while I wait for the translation it is the emotion, energy, and intensity with which she speaks that I am feeling. She was born on this land, with her parents here before her. She raised her family here, although they are all gone now. After she buried her husband and two children, the other children left to find jobs.

There are no jobs, and no schooling for them here, and she wants them to have a better life. When the dams are built her land will be flooded. The company has promised to build her a new house on the ridge beyond the river, with electricity and running water. She plans to dig up the bones of her family herself and re-bury them on her new land.

She hopes that when the power comes, there will be jobs and some of her sons will come home to work on the construction. If the project doesn't happen, she will die here once it gets too hard for her to grow vegetables. The idea of running water and electricity is a luxury she can hardly imagine.

Different People, Same Beauty

Days later, I'm in another small community in Patagonia, standing in a barn with Juan (not his real name), a union organizer for local farmers. The smell of manure and the lowing of the cows blows around us while he tells me that no one is listening to his members.

The farmers he represents work desperately hard to put food on the tables for their families, and their livestock are often being killed by the pumas that Conservation Patagonia protects on their land. When they complain to the Conservation Foundation, they are told that is what nature intended, but he thinks nature intended for people to eat before puma populations are expanded.

The loss of one sheep can mean months of food for a family and represents wages that can't be replaced for the farmer. If the area opens up with the dams, there will be more opportunities for local people.

Very Different Perspectives and Worldviews on What Is Happening

He tells me that those who are against the project are Americans, funded by the wealthy who want this place to stay the same, like they want the people to stay the same as if they are quaint artifacts of a time long gone. He says they think they have the right to speak for the local people, but they aren't even from here. They just fly in on their planes, stay on the conservation foundation lands, and fly out again. They buy up more and more land every year, so that local people can't earn a living and must go to the cities and towns to find work.

More People, More Perspectives

Later, I'm standing in the corner of the lobby in the local hotel, witnessing the excitement and intensity of Flora, (not her real name), as she tells me that she has had enough people from away coming to tell Patagonians what they want. The irony of me being from far away is not lost on me but is not registering with her.

Grassroots Movement Striving to Have Their Voices Heard

She is pushing posters and bumper stickers into my hands, asking me to sign her petition. She has organized a grassroots association, valiantly standing up for the rights of local people, demanding that their voices be heard.

They want Patagonia protected and free, and they want opportunities and growth. She says it is people like Douglas and Kris Tompkins (both of them former executives at the Patagonia clothing company and the two of them founders of Conservation Patagonia), who are using their money to keep the people of Patagonia small so they can fly in with their planes and say how lovely the wilderness is, before they fly back to their American mansions. She says they don't care about her or the community here, they don't interact with them, they don't care if there are no schools, no jobs, or no electricity.

While the Tompkins have funded a global resistance campaign of 'Patagonia sin Represas' (Patagonia without dams), her small group has produced their own campaign; 'Patagonia sin Tompkins' (Patagonia without Tompkins).

Power and Influence Used for Personal Benefit

It occurs to me that it doesn't matter where you go in the world, those who hold power and influence wield it to benefit themselves.

No matter where this work takes me, I hold the same conversations over and over again – this deep yearning to be heard, to be seen, and to be understood. This deep human desire to be valued and worthy, and to make something of our lives for ourselves and our children.

The Tension Between the Haves and Have-Nots, and Who Has the Money to Be Heard

There is a deep, systemic challenge where money and the power and influence it represents speaks as if it speaks for all, as if it represents the interests of those who are affected, and yet mostly it doesn't. Conversation Patagonia, the Tompkins, Greenpeace, or Save our Rivers isn't speaking for Maria or Juan or Flora, and the thousands like them around the globe.

It's unusual that this situation isn't about the money, power, and influence of multinational corporations who are harvesting natural resources for profit. In this case, the money, power, and influence are held by people who want to protect the environment – over the people who live there.

Don't get me wrong, I'm all for preserving sacred spaces and the environment, but I'm wondering how we do this AND support the human beings in those places to achieve their goals, to develop and prosper, and make lives better for their children? Can we not do both at the same time?

Courage to Question Power and Influence as a Revolutionary Act

We seem to have come to this place and time where everything is an either / or equation with winners and losers, and inevitably the winners have more money, power, and influence than the losers.

What if instead we chose to solve challenges based on all of us prospering as we move forward?

I had a conversation with a friend one day. She referenced an article where the author had suggested that those who are loudest and most vocal about projects in their communities, those who shouted most about "NIMBY" are the new revolutionaries. I think perhaps we could look at it another way – often those who lead the NIMBY calls to action are protecting the status quo, defending the privilege, power, and influence they already hold, stopping outsiders from encroaching on their territory. I think revolutionaries are those who call out and question the status quo, who make power and influence evident, and who raise their voices to be heard, advocating for the change they want to see in the world.

In the end, all humans want the same things. We want a home, people to love, an opportunity for a better life for our families and communities, connection and belonging, and to be seen.

It doesn't matter where you go, the hope and need are the same.

The challenge is that the conversations we are having around the globe are highlighting one set of voices and marginalizing another set. We are talking, but we aren't listening.

Impossible Situations Are Everywhere

A few years ago, I was hired by a Canadian federal government department to work with a group of staff to build their capacity for brave, honest conversations. It's what I do, and the call to do the work was simple enough on the surface. At first, I wasn't told a lot of details, only that I would be preparing a group of staff to enter into extremely emotional, controversial conversations with communities on behalf of the Government of Canada. To be in alignment with my own integrity, I needed to know more about the situation, history, and expectations before I said yes.

Finally, the department shared that I was being asked to help prepare a group of staff who would enter into consultations with First Nation communities along the length of the Trans Mountain pipeline.

Let me tell you a brief history of the Trans Mountain (TMX) pipeline so you can start to weave the threads of complexity together*.

- In Canada, the pipeline was built to carry oil from Alberta to Vancouver (Burnaby) B.C., in the 1950s.
- There were a number of oil spills over the years, including a significant spill in the 1980s.
- It was expanded through Jasper National Park and Mount Robson Provincial Park in the early 2000s. These are places of pristine and fragile natural environment.
- An additional expansion was planned in 2012, but extremely strong public opposition emerged, including arrests, protests, and national and international advocacy campaigns.
- In 2016, the federal government announced all pipeline projects will now be reviewed in part on the greenhouse gas emissions

produced, and that proponents must improve consultations with First Nations.

- In 2016, the federal government approved the pipeline, subject to 157 conditions. There were multiple appeals filed against the decision, including staunch opposition from the B.C. provincial government, and countless protests, blockades, and arrests.
- In 2018, the Canadian federal government decided to buy the pipeline and expansion project from Kinder Morgan Canada for $4.5 billion, after the company suspended work on the pipeline due to challenges and opposition. The government justified the purchase as being in the national interest.
- Between August and November 2018, the federal court of appeal overturned the government approval of the pipeline expansion, saying the project review was so flawed it could not be relied on as a basis for decision. The government said it would undertake a new environmental assessment process with focus on the impact of oil tankers on killer whales and to improve consultations with First Nations.
- In June 2019, the federal government approved the expansion of the pipeline a second time.
  *Summarized from reports by the CBC: https://www.cbc.ca/news/canada/calgary/timeline-key-dates-history-trans-mountain-pipeline-1.4849370

I was hired in November 2018, right after government approval of the pipeline was overturned by the courts, amidst political announcements that a new environmental assessment process would be conducted that would improve consultation with First Nations, and look more carefully at the environmental impacts, including those on killer whales.

A Personal Ethical Dilemma

In principle, I don't take work on pipelines or oil and gas projects. My values feel so out of alignment with supporting work that expands resource extraction with large negative environmental, and social impacts. I don't judge others for doing this work; I just don't want to do it myself. However, I have worked for a few oil and gas and energy companies on wind energy projects, or to improve relationships with local indigenous communities.

Once I knew what I was being asked to do and what project it was for I agonized over whether to accept the work. In the end, I decided that while I didn't personally support the expansion of the pipeline, or the choice of the federal government to purchase a pipeline with taxpayer dollars, I did believe in the importance of meaningful conversations with indigenous communities. If I could be of service to supporting staff in that goal, I would be acting in alignment with my own values. As we considered in Part 1, when I consider that leadership starts with me, having clarity on my values so I can make choices that keep me in alignment is a core leadership competency.

When the Problem Is Defined Differently

I was hired to design and deliver training in brave, honest conversations to thirty staff who would work with indigenous communities along the TMX line. That's what my contract said.

However, that wasn't what I ended up doing.

I walked into a meeting room on a snowy November morning, ready to deliver training on how to have really difficult, high heat conversations about the pipeline in indigenous communities. I was clear that my role wasn't to tell people how to engage with indigenous communities. That isn't my area of expertise, and I would never presume to suggest I could train on that knowledge. What I could do was teach people how to get better at having conversations that matter.

What Is Really Going on Here?

Except, it turned out that I learned pretty quickly that this room of thirty federal staff people already had relationships with the communities they were being sent to, had decades of experience in having these conversations, and had been trained countless times with skills and knowledge to work in conflict. I was scheduled for four days of work with this team, and it became clear by mid-morning on day one that every plan and design for training I had was going to have to be re-worked. This group was open to learning new skills and ways of being but more than anything they wanted to talk about:

- Their fear and anxiety that they were being sent into an impossible situation where they would engage meaningfully with indigenous communities, and then everything they negotiated would have to be sent back to Ottawa and fed up the hierarchical chain to the Prime Minister's office, and then come back down again, with marching orders they would have to follow in next steps, with a lack of context, understanding, or relationship with those in the communities.
- Their knowledge that the timelines laid out by the political powers were insufficient for meaningful consultation, and lacking in respect for cultural protocols, building trust, or strengthening relationships with local communities.
- That they had been equipped with a task without the authority, decision-making, or accountability structure in place that would allow them to be successful.
- That their own values and commitments to meaningful engagement were hugely out of alignment with the work they were being tasked to do.
- That the whole activity would potentially damage and harm relationships and trust with indigenous communities along the pipeline, and those impacts would permanently damage their own reputations and ability to do the work they were most committed to.
- That the decision had already been made, and this was an exercise in futility; and
- That they would fail and be blamed for anything that went wrong.

These are BIG fears and worries and they crowded out any space for training or learning.

When Systems, Structures and Values Are Out of Alignment

They also point to the complexity of the work in this space – so often a brave, honest conversation isn't just a conversation. It is needed because our systems, structures, and internal values are all out of alignment. If we are being tasked with one thing, without consideration of how all things are interconnected in a complex system, we will fail, eroding trust, democracy, and relationships.

You can't task a group of people to conduct meaningful consultation with another group of people if the system is designed around command and control, hierarchy, and an unclear, untransparent, murky decision-making process.

You can't call for meaningful consultation and enact timelines that don't permit relationships to be built, trust to be restored, and issues to be negotiated in good faith. Words and actions must align.

Reflect and Practice – Seeking Patterns and Insights

Consider a complex situation that seems stuck or impossible to find traction or forward momentum. Step back and stop focusing on the details. Ask yourself these questions, and brainstorm everything you can think of that falls into each category.

- What is happening here that is positive, affirming, or building momentum towards the future we want?
- What opportunities might exist, or that we can leverage if we address them effectively?
- What is happening now that is having a negative impact, causing tension, conflict, or challenges now, and possibly into the future?
- What is going on that is creating tension or challenges that if we address them, we could create positive momentum?

Once you've got data and input from multiple sources and perspectives for each question, look for themes and patterns.

Are there similarities?

Are there tensions or differences in one category that impact another category?

Who needs to be in this conversation so you can fully see and understand what is happening, and who needs to be part of what happens next?

Then consider where to go from there.

Reflect and practice – Influencing Change

A core competency of any leader is the capacity to influence change. Note that I didn't say the capacity to persuade, convince, or educate people about why or how they should change. I want to place emphasis on our capacity for influence. We often think that influence is a dirty word, but it goes to the intention of our actions related to influence. In its simplest form, influence is about having a positive impact on the behaviour, thinking, or actions of others.

- **Ask, don't tell.** A lack of control, a sense of coercion or manipulation, losing autonomy – all of these things increase resistance to change. Instead, ask people about their fears, concerns, or worries. Ask them about their lived experiences and needs. Ask them how they define the challenge, and how they would solve the problem. Emphasize relationship over action in the beginning, so connection is established. Once that connection is established, resistance to change will lessen, and you will have a deeper understanding of the impacts of change.
- **Invite and evoke empathy.** Encourage people to consider the costs and consequences of the status quo on others through storytelling, sharing circles, video interviews, and more. When people can see beyond their own immediate reactions and concerns, they can begin to see there are others in their organization, community, or

group who also have needs, and some might be different than their own. This creates an appetite and receptivity for potential change.

- **Create an experience and a conversation about the change.** People are most likely to change their opinions through a combination of personal experience and conversation. So, create an experience that exposes them to something new and different, and have a conversation with others about that experience. This is the basis for neuroplasticity, which allows our brains to change and grow. Novelty, memorability, relationship, personal relevance – these things create the conditions for people to change their thinking and learn new things.

- **Speak truth to power.** Apply your deep commitment to what you stand for, leverage your strengths, and call people in (instead of call people out) where change is crucial. Be authentic, passionate, and committed to your vision, and to them at the same time. Take a stand for the change that needs to happen.

- **Create a sense of collective action.** When we give people something to be for, rather than something to be against, we leverage the highest positive form of energy in emotion: hope. Invite people to be part of solving the challenge, taking a stand, and creating positive change.

Identify a situation where you are experiencing resistance from others. Consciously choose a different way of interacting, focusing on participation, diverse perspectives, compassion, hope, and possibility. Reflect on what worked and what to continue to work on.

CHAPTER 17

The Unicorn of Collaboration

Sometimes, you come across a group of people who you expect to be entrenched in deep, rigid conflict, yet they are like a unicorn in a magical forest, talking together over the years on different sides of a polarized issue, finding a way forward. This NGO I've been working with is like that unicorn.

It is a voluntary, self-organizing group of people who all care about animal welfare. The group includes farmers, agricultural producers, folks who process and sell animal products, animal welfare advocacy groups, veterinarians, academics and researchers, and government representatives – all working together to create guidelines and voluntary codes of compliance to ensure the humane treatment of animals.

They are passionate, committed, and hard working in their shared interest. They come back to the table again and again to make progress and talk about issues where they see things totally differently. They keep working to create a space where the unicorn thrives.

The Last Few Years Have Been Difficult for Everyone

Over the last few years, things have gotten harder for all of them. Societal expectations have increased pressure on all the groups, and each representative at the table has an organization to report back to, and some of those organizations have firm positions on issues under discussion. Some of those positions are on very different sides of the conversation, and that means that finding agreement or a way forward can fade away, and relationships can fray in the process.

The definition of humane treatment of animals, increasing clarity, and renewing agreement on their shared values, and controversial, polarizing issues like whether fur farming is considered by all members to be an acceptable practice, have been slowing them down and creating tension. Discussion on some of the voluntary codes of practice for animal care have stalled out as some participants in the discussion take hard lines, unwilling to find compromise on both sides, and relationships and trust have eroded.

Eventually, even though they had years of great work under their belts, the tension and challenges became great enough that they began to question whether they could move forward together, or if there was a future for the magical creature that was their organization.

Years ago, I had given a speech at a conference they held about working in collaborative ways on high stakes issues. They remembered it, and called me to ask if I could help guide them to find a way forward. It wasn't a guarantee there would be a way forward. My work was to map the sources of the conflict and help them have conversations to conclude on where to go next.

Knowing the Value of Brave, Honest Conversations Doesn't Make Them Easier

It isn't often I have the privilege of working with a group of people already steeped in the benefits and possibilities of brave, honest conversations – this group is living proof that people on different sides of a highly polarized issue can work together with shared goals over a long period of time. Yet, here they were, struggling to agree, challenged by relationships, mistrust, and challenging topics of discussion.

We can believe in and practice the work of brave, honest conversations and still find ourselves mired in challenges and conflict. This is true in our lives, organizations and communities. This work is imperfect, messy and a place of constant learning. The awareness that there is work to do, relationships to strengthen, and trust to build is the first step to de-escalating conflict.

When I began leading conversations with members of the group, tensions surfaced. Trust had been damaged through words, actions, and behaviours on many sides. Those not directly involved were hesitant to step in, uncertain how to proceed. Others stepped back, believing the challenges were the doing of others. Some people had dug into their position or view, certain they were right, and others were wrong, losing sight of shared values and goals. Some believed it was time to re-examine the organization's values and goals, while others held tightly to what had worked in the past. Some were ready to re-make the way they made decisions, looking to majority rule, while others wanted to refine their dialogue-based consensus process. This is a perfect example of what happens in countless organizations, groups and relationships.

Those are the topics under discussion at this organization, but it turns out even when the topics are different, what people really need to talk about can be similar.

Organizations Differ, But Leadership Lessons Are Similar

I work with organizations, leadership teams, and staff who want to change the way they work together, and change the way they work with partners, stakeholders, and community external to their organizations. When they hire me, it is usually because of a crisis situation, where everything is going poorly, they feel under siege and the stakes are high. While all organizations are different, the leadership lessons they experience are hauntingly similar.

What is happening inside our organizations echoes outside our organizations in the perceptions, credibility, and reputation of our organization in the community and world.

Organizations are entities on their own, but they are made up of human beings. It is the human beings who feel under siege, conflicted, objects of distrust and inadequacy.

It is the human beings who make the culture of the organization, regardless of what is stated in the organization's values, mission, and vision. It is where our behaviours, actions, mindset, and beliefs come to life and enable us to work from our strengths, perform with purpose, and feel valued and worthy. Or, where we feel like a spoke in a wheel, without purpose or value, and sometimes worse, blamed for the organization's perception, credibility, and trust challenges.

In another organization I'm working with, I was hired to help them build a stronger team by identifying sources of internal conflict and building capacity to learn to talk together better. This organization is a US state environmental agency, and many staff are highly trained technical experts like environmental scientists, engineers, and public health professionals. Their expertise runs deep, and they were fully committed to protecting the environment and public health. While I could help them see the topics that were causing the conflict they were experiencing, what they were initially blind to, were the tensions inside their organization.

- A culture of risk aversion and an emphasis on the priority value of technical expertise was contributing to a culture of fear, a need for perfection, and valuing of facts and data over lived experiences, feelings, and perceptions.
- A fear of getting things wrong was stifling innovation and creating an environment of blame and shame where employees were afraid to speak up, fix problems, or raise issues.
- A siloed and hierarchical organizational structure meant that leadership made decisions in ways that were opaque to staff, and staff sent issues up the decision-making chain to never hear the outcome of them. It created levels of distrust, suspicion, and anxiety throughout the organization, and contributed to staff protecting territory, relationships, and resources.
- Overwhelmed, under siege employees were exhausted, burnt out, fearful and worried, with low motivation.

Like all things, there are two parts to this environment. While everything I have noted is true for this organization, what is also true is that:

- Leadership and staff are deeply committed to the mandate and vision of the organization, and value the opportunity to work and make a positive impact in communities.
- There are common values across the organization – equity, compassion, working hard, doing the right thing, demonstrating credibility and trustworthiness.
- There is a deep yearning and desire to work collaboratively, to break down barriers and find solutions to difficult problems, to create a work environment where everyone feels valued and worthy and to get things 'right.'
- There is enormous untapped expertise in the organization waiting to be explored and expanded.

The challenges inside the organization are being echoed and mirrored outside the organization with the clients and communities they work with, resulting in a perception by some of a lack of care and trustworthiness, tension, and strained relationships with stakeholders, and resistance to interacting or working with the agency.

On the Surface Everything Seems Different

The two organizations I reference couldn't be more different on the surface. One, an NGO with members from a wide diversity of experience and perspective with a long history of working collaboratively, amidst external and social pressures. And the other organization a state agency with clear mandate, commitment to making a difference, full of technical experts, and structured, hierarchical decision-making grappling to achieve their mandate amidst systemic challenges.

You wouldn't think these organizations would be similar, but the lessons and approaches that create the change both organizations are looking for are remarkably aligned.

In both organizations, we worked together to implement a series of strategies designed to bring out the very best in people, build relationships and trust, and increase capacity to talk together, knowing that when these things were in place, they could tackle other difficult challenges together. The strategies implemented in both organizations include:

- **Acknowledge, own, and take responsibility for the tensions, challenges, and conflict** – Based on the premise that leadership begins with you, every participant was encouraged to build some self-awareness through reflection and understanding of impact versus intention to unpack and own their own role in the challenges being experienced in the organization through a series of individual and group exercises and coaching.

- **Build capacity, skills, knowledge, and ways of being for talking together about tough topics** – We don't know what we don't know, and no one is born knowing how to have brave, honest conversations. Building skills, knowledge, and ways of being to talk about important and challenging things is crucial. You can be skilled technical experts, passionate in your views and values, but if you don't know how to approach or participate in a brave, honest conversation it is likely to not go well. Even in a group with experience and skills in this area, growing tensions, hurt, and perceptions about each other can get in the way of talking together. Workshops, training sessions, and practice opportunities formed the basis of building the necessary capacity.

- **Value the humanity in each of us** – Authenticity, leading from and leveraging individual and group strengths, celebrating differences, inviting diversity, and cultivating empathy; these are ways of being that enable groups to face difficulty and come through more connected, performing better. However, when the layers of tension and hurt have built up like sediment, it takes time to dig down to re-establish a relationship. Coaching, guided group conversations, and short practice sessions, create an environment where people slowly shift from holding the story they are telling themselves, to a new story about the people they are interacting with.

- **Build comfort with emotion** – We've been trained to believe that it is unprofessional to have feelings at work, and to reward rationality over emotions. Unfortunately, that myth results in people bringing half themselves to work, and resentments, frustrations, hurt, and fear get buried under the surface of group interactions. This breeds an organizational culture that slowly bends towards perfectionism, blame, fear, and allied camps. When we recognize that people perform best when they bring their whole selves to the undertaking, we create deeper understanding, connection, trust, and relationships, and we leverage strength, purpose, and commitment to do good work. This takes training, education, and a new way of working together, reinforced through coaching and reflection.

- **Connect to values and strengths, and lead from a heart-centered place to improve performance and results** – When you practice leveraging individual strengths, rather than building processes and procedures that require everyone to be the same, you build organizations where people shine, rely on each other, and celebrate differences. This leads to innovation, creativity, problem solving, and improved team performance.

- **Take actions and strategies personally and organizationally that build trust, increase connection, and deepen understanding, so that difficult problems can be solved** – Once all the other strategies are in place, you need an action plan and an operational plan. Specific goals and objectives about what you will do differently, backed up by ways of working that prioritize reflection, talking together, and valuing differences and strengths are crucial. You can build capacity and then slowly find your organization back in the same old way of working together that created tension, conflict, and low performance. It takes intention, conscious choice, and prioritizing compassion in our work. This looks like standing agenda items focused on reflection and connection, prioritizing conversations about difficult topics in teams, leadership, and throughout the organization, ongoing practices of reflection and learning about what is working and what could be improved.

These strategies can feel counterintuitive and uncomfortable because they are different from the linear, rational, compartmentalized ways we've been taught to work in organizations. Those ways lower performance and effectiveness and take a human toll over time.

Implementing a different way, generates increased performance and results, and human beings who are motivated, engaged, and connected to their work.

What Does it Take to Build Trust?

There are no simple, easy steps, checklists, or guidebooks to building trust, especially when it has been damaged, eroded, or destroyed. We need trust for our relationships to thrive, our institutions to function, and for a stable society. We see around the globe how the lack of trust in the systems and structures that underpin society are affected.

Because there are no simple, easy solutions, I come back to the choices we each make as leaders. It starts with you – your actions, choices, and the ways you show up in the world impacts trust around you. Let's start there to focus on trust and expand it out like ripples in a lake.

A Model for Building Trust

I believe there are four pillars to building trust:

1. **Focus on strengthening relationships** – When we do this, we demonstrate generosity, effort, respect, and the time required to foster and build relationships. When relationships are present, we can talk about hard things and find solutions together.
2. **Build social connection** – When we respect and honour diversity and identity, we honour and value other people, bearing witness to their needs and experience, recognizing the humanity and inter-connection we all share. When we do this, we build community, decreasing isolation and disconnection, fostering strong webs of resilience between people.
3. **Create spaces of interactive, empowered participation** – When we utilize the recipes to create spaces of collaboration, we increase

equity, address power imbalances, and see the whole landscape of patterns and possibilities that allow us to find solutions to complex challenges.

4. **Demonstrate integrity** – When we act from a place of authenticity and transparency, taking full responsibility for our impact on each other, we deepen understanding, and through commitment build credibility and a perception that we are in this together.

Taken together, these four pillars build strong trust in our lives, organizations, and communities.

Reflect and Practice – Building Trust

Leadership requires a mix of DOING (actions), and BEING (mindset), and they weave together to create effective leadership. Review the four pillars of building trust and ask yourself:

-   What will you DO? What actions can you take that will build trust in your work and life?
-   How will you BE? What mindset will you hold to support you to build trust in your work and life?

Reflect and Practice – Building a Culture of Engagement

The first step to building a culture of engagement is to understand what culture you have now. To start, you can conduct interviews or a survey with members of the organization.

Make sure you consider power dynamics that may impact people's willingness to be totally truthful about their experiences when you undertake this task, or you may only reveal half the picture. I often commit to anonymity – that the results of the interviews or survey will not be released to anyone at any time to support full sharing and participation.

Ask questions like the ones outlined below to begin to understand your existing culture and sources of challenge, tension, and conflict, and where change is needed.

- What has your experience been working with the organization? Can you share a personal story, example or experience that highlights the essence of your experience?
- Have you experienced any personal challenges or concerns? If so, what are they?
- Have you experienced any positive or affirming interactions? If so, what are they?
- Please complete the following statement: For me, my work with the organization is a success when….
- Comparing your experience to that of the ideal situation, what issues or concerns do you have?
- In your experience, how well does the team work together? What is positive? What is challenging?
- What are your experiences working across teams in terms of communication, roles, responsibilities, or other requirements?
- How comfortable are you sharing your hopes, concerns, and experiences with other staff? Why is that?
- In an ideal situation, what are your hopes or expectations for how relationships and group dynamics would work in the organization?
- If you were to look down the road and imagine the future work environment and dynamics of the team, what do you hope to see?
- In the future, how do you see yourself working with others, including those with views different than your own?
- What would you like others to know about you, your experience, and hopes?
- What do you need in order to participate in a conversation with other members of the organization on these issues?

Once you've got survey or interview results, analyze the data, and identify themes. Share the summary with everyone and begin a conversation about what resonates or is surprising or challenging for them.

Then slowly begin implementing strategies that will shift you towards a culture of collaboration, compassion, connection, and innovation.

CHAPTER 18

Lead With a Wide-Open Heart

"Everyone tells you to armour up when you enter the public arena and to get a really thick skin. I think you need to do the opposite. I think it requires a relentlessly open heart to lead in the public arena." That was said by Mayor Lisa Helps of Victoria, B.C., when I asked what her best advice is for people doing work in the public arena.

Her words echo in my head – what does it mean to be relentlessly open-hearted? Is compassion, love, kindness, and the courage to show up that way enough to combat the complexity, chaos, polarization, and conflict of the public arena?

I've come to believe the answer is yes. Choose an open mind, lead with an open heart, show up with compassion, kindness, and courage. It sounds simple, but maybe we've made everything else way too complicated. Sometimes the best solutions are the simplest. And sometimes simple is also really hard to do.

We make sense of the world and find meaning for ourselves in stories. The following experience became a story that shaped how I lead high conflict, high emotion situations.

We are sitting in a musty room in an old convent, people gathered in groups of five and six, leaning on tables sipping tea, and murmuring quietly. The room is full of hundreds of members of the Inuit community living in Ottawa, Canada, brought together to share their history and experiences with the impacts of colonization.

Bearing Witness

My job is to hold the space for this conversation, and to gently guide the sharing around the room, to be sure the stories are captured so they can be witnessed. Chronicling a people's history and experiences with the impacts of colonization sounds as though we could make a list of the impacts or sanitize a hundred years of pain and suffering onto a flip chart.

In reality, it is the opposite of that.

It is stories of heartache, tragedy, and trauma. It is tears of grief and sadness, of children being taken away, houses bulldozed, of being treated with disdain, and disrespect as less than human.

It is the pain of being stripped of identity, of being told you are wrong, and yet holding to your beliefs, values, and culture, despite the hardship.

It is every bad thing one human has done to another, all in the name of colonisation.

Experiences are recited quietly by the people gathered together, offered slowly and tenderly as speaking of the pain deepens the wounds.

Words are received with loving kindness and a calm acceptance by others – these people see each other's pain because they've felt it too.

The Room Feels Close and Tender

People cry, comforted by others. People get angry, and others respectfully listen and honour the rage. The conversation goes in waves-- cresting with pain and heartache, to subside into gentle acknowledgement, occasionally broken by a joke or funny comment. *"You have to find laughter every day,"* says one participant, the implication being that without it, you can't continue.

What Does Healing Look Like?

At some point I ask the group, *"What does healing look like? How do you move forward?"*

This conversation is part of the work of the Qikiqtani Truth Commission, and elders have tasked us with reconciling the difficult path forward. It is a simple question to ask, and I witness that it is a difficult question to answer.

One participant reflects deeply, and then powerfully says, *"If we cannot forgive, we cannot move forward. We do not forget, but we work together for a better future."*

The Gift of Holding Space

Years later, I look back on this moment in my career, at the gift of holding space for these conversations. I think about how this work shifted and changed my perspective on the leadership that is needed in the public arena now, and on the space that must be created for us to talk about the hardest of things, together, with open hearts and open minds. These conversations, in this dusty room in Ottawa, laid the seeds of what I call Brave, Honest Conversations.

We Have a Long Hard Road Ahead of Us

For the complex challenges facing us there are no easy solutions. This is an exceptional, unprecedented time to live in. At other times in history there have been leaders facing one or two, or even a few complex challenges all at once. At no time in history has the list of interconnected, systemic challenges been this long. There is no easy way out, and no quick fix this time.

Democracy requires great courage. Courage to speak your mind AND hear the voices of others. To seek to understand the views and perspectives of people who are the same as you, AND of people who are different from you. It is not about gathering those who think like you and confirming with each other that your view is the 'right' one. Democracy wasn't designed for voting-it was designed for deliberation, for citizens to come together and weigh complex issues, and debate how to move forward together – and then to vote after that process of conversation is complete.

Talking Together Is a Practice That Creates Connection and a Way Forward

When we don't talk about the hard things in our families, organizations, and communities, we don't grow, change, or make progress. We must hold our tensions and differences and find ways to talk about them.

It is a fallacy that if we do not have conflict that we are all safe and fine, and relieved from our suffering. If we sweep it under the carpet, and avoid and hide from it, we aren't better off – we are less than we could be, and we have lost the chance for growth, learning, and for the collective good.

The truth is, if we talk about our differences, if we truly understand each other, if we stop demonizing each other and drawing lines in the sand, we might be able to come together to solve the complex problems we face.

There Is a Different Way

The answer is inside each one of us. At the same time that there is strife and challenge, there is connection, hope, and understanding being created in communities everywhere.

There are people seeing each other, shifting their understanding, choosing to work together with others who are different from themselves, to find ways forward together.

There is divide and polarization, and also a deep human yearning for connection.

There are complex problems, and also the resilient human spirit.

There are challenges, and there are also opportunities. These poles are two parts of a whole.

When we sit complacent or silent, or we talk only to those who agree with us or have the same views, we contribute to the challenges we face. When we choose to have a voice and use it for the collective good, we are part of action for change.

After decades of work in the public arena doing community engagement, I know the system is not working. Yes, people have a right to a voice, and when decisions are made those decisions should reflect and consider that voice. Projects should gather the insight from a variety of voices in an inclusive way, and people should have the information they need to participate meaningfully. However, in so many ways we are focusing our conversations on the easy stuff, the simple stuff.

We're mostly not talking together about hate crimes, racism, gun violence, or the harm we're causing the planet.

We're not teaching people to speak to each other with love, to reach out and seek connection, common ground, and solution. In fact, we're teaching people to demand what they want as the solution at all costs, and that the answer is in shouting about what they DON'T want, not what they DO want.

We've eroded trust in government, decision-making, and even the media to the point that we don't know which way to turn.

I say 'we' purposely because aren't we the people who participate in change processes, or choose instead to sit back and comment on Facebook?

Aren't 'we' the ones who protest and also demonize the other side who are in the role of decision-maker, but who check the box on gathering citizen, employee, or stakeholder input so we can say we did, and then do what we planned anyway?

These are OUR communities and organizations, and we need to choose differently.

It breaks my heart and moves me to tears. It calls me to action to know I've got no choice but to be part of building something new and different, where we hold the really tough conversations bravely and honestly, with space for all of us as we find solutions together.

Make a Choice to Be Part of Creating Something Different

When we make a choice to be part of a brave, honest conversation about the tough challenges in our world, we open the door to possibility by talking to people who are different from us. Those who hold different values and views, who see the world through different eyes, and have different experiences.

You can't change the world with your Facebook friends, but you might be able to change the world by opening your mind to different views so you can help find solutions that work for all of us.

When you choose to let go of assumptions and open your heart, you can engage with people you are thinking of right now as the enemy, or as wrong, or evil.

You can let go of your need to be right or to win, and recognize we inhabit one small planet, we all live here, and it is in all of our interests to solve the challenges that face us.

There is no winning if some of us lose.

When you acknowledge your fear and discomfort and choose to stay in tough conversations to find a way forward, you embody courage, and choose leadership over the mob. When you reach out to someone whose values are different from yours, who you are in conflict with, and bravely say, 'Let's talk,' you allow for a different future than the conflict trodden path you are walking now.

A New Kind of Leadership

Look around you – in your organization, community, and on the world stage. What examples of leadership do you see? What does it look like when leaders create a positive impact on others and the space around them? What does it look like when solutions are found to complex challenges and people move forward together? What does it look like when leaders create the opposite experience? What is the difference?

We've got two opposite and contradictory examples of leadership playing out in the global public arena: leaders who act out blame, shame, divide, and fear mongering; and leaders who call forth compassion, empathy, and a sense of the collective. There remains a sense that leaders must be 'strong' and that talk of love, compassion, and kindness is 'weak'.

Leaders who bring out the best from us, and who call the best from themselves are the leaders we need now in the public arena.

We need a new kind of leadership. Leaders who show up, stand up, and bravely step forward to solve the problems we face.

"No one is born hating another person because of the color of his skin, or his background, or his religion. People must learn to hate, and if they can learn to hate, they can be taught to love, for love comes more naturally to the human heart than its opposite."

~Nelson Mandela

The answer is in each of us, in how we want to lead our lives, in how we want to show up, and in how we come together to address the challenges we face. If you can lean into love, you can evoke it in the space of the most important conversations of your life.

The answer is in an army of brave leaders who choose hope, connection, and possibility.

The answer is in leaders willing to have brave conversations about the things that matter, conversations that create space for everyone, not just the folks who agree with them.

Let me go back to that moment in that room in Ottawa, holding space for members of the Inuit community to dive deeply into the impacts of colonization, and to explore the seeds of healing.

Those moments planted this idea in me that this work of being in community together, of being in conversation with each other, is far more than getting a project built or moving a program forward.

It is less about checking a box to say people were consulted, and more about engaging with our fellow humanity to be there for each other so we can move forward together.

It isn't about managing or resolving conflict, instead it is about transforming the conflict into something that is entirely different, charting a new path forward.

As Mayor Lisa Helps says, it is being relentlessly open-hearted in our conversations with each other, believing we can do hard things together when we are deeply connected.

I believe that when we have brave, honest conversations, we create connection, build trust, strengthen relationships, and deepen understanding. When those things are present, anything is possible. When we see each other's humanity, we can step into complex challenges and co-create possible new futures.

And that takes leadership. A different kind of leadership than the traditional models of leadership we see so often.

A Model of Courageous Leadership

I've come to believe that courageous leaders excel in four core competencies.

A competency is a skill, knowledge, and/or way of being that enables performance and effectiveness. Too often we focus on skills and knowledge, without recognizing that ways of being, behaviours, and characteristics, are as integral to the impact we create as what we know or what we do. In this case, competencies are focused on leadership in the public arena.

A Model of Courageous Leadership

Let's consider the model of Courageous Leadership in more depth.

Commitment and Faith

As with all things involving leadership, leading brave, honest conversations in the public arena begins with you. Deep self-awareness and emotional intelligence are core to transforming tough issues into solutions.

- What do you believe in?
- What do you value?
- What orientation do you hold towards conflict, emotion, discomfort?
- How strong is your faith that talking together about the most difficult things to find solutions is possible?
- When you lead, are you acting in ways that are in alignment with your values, beliefs, and faith?

COURAGEOUS LEADERSHIP MODEL

Courageous Leaders have strong capacity in all four core competencies & are constantly checking in with themselves about:

- The conscious choice they are making to lead
- Acting from full permission for authenticity
- Aligning their choices with their values
- Taking responsibility for the impact of their leadership

INCREASING COMMITMENT AND COURAGE >>

INTEGRITY & COURAGE

Advocating For Values

Standing For Something Important

Positive Impact And Perception Of Credibility

INFLUENCE & ENROLLING

Inspiring & Empowering Participation

Building A Movement

Creating A Clear Choice

COMMITMENT & FAITH

Mindset And Orientation

Core Beliefs

Acting In Alignment With Values

OPENNESS & CONNECTION

Tools & Methods Of Engagement

Experience That Is Created

Space Of The Conversation

INCREASING CONNECTION & INFLUENCE >>

WWW.BRAVELYLEAD.COM

When you are clear on these things and take action grounded from this place, you create a powerful resonance and congruence that you are credible, and people can rely on your actions to align with your words.

When you excel at Commitment and Courage you build positivity and possibility around the most difficult of situations, growing the commitment of others to stay the course.

Openness and Connection

This is often where traditional emphasis is placed in the work of conversational leadership.

- Are you a good facilitator?
- Can you ask powerful questions?
- Do you know how to employ tools, methods, and structures that support the conversation?
- Can you work effectively with the ebb and flow of emotion in a brave, honest conversation to find the meaning that results in transformation?
- Do you create a space where people feel seen and heard?
- Are you working with what is inside of people, and also what is swirling in their communities or organization, and in society, around the topic of discussion?

When you excel at the Openness and Connection competency you build community, intimacy, and momentum for change.

Integrity and Courage

This competency is one often lacking in a world of sound bites, short-term thinking and decisions based on supporting those who hold power and influence. The lack of trust in governments, the media, and the private sector is a testament to low levels of competency in this pillar among many in leadership roles in the public arena.

- What do you stand for?
- What are you committed to creating in the world?
- What do you advocate for and put your energy towards building and changing?
- What behaviours and leadership characteristics do you demonstrate (think of humility, empathy, authenticity, and others of the seven characteristics that have a positive impact)?
- What impact do you have on those around you, and are you taking responsibility for that impact?

- Do you make choices and decisions that are open, transparent, and clear?
- Are your motives and interests evident and transparent to people?
- Can you stand in the fire of public opinion, grounded by your own values and commitments, and to make difficult decisions?

When you excel at the Integrity and Courage competency, you combat the fear and uncertainty that inevitably arises in challenging situations and demonstrate trustworthiness and credibility.

Influence and Enrolling

This competency is the space where courage, authenticity, commitment, and skill weave together, where your faith in possibility, and your actions in alignment with values is evident.

- Do you hold a vision of the change you are seeking to create?
- Does your vision have space for others to see themselves in it, and do you generate hope and momentum that inspires action?
- Are you clear about the choices and actions others can take to activate change?
- Do you give people something to be for (rather than something to be against)?
- Are you actively seeking out partners and participants, growing the conversation beyond those who think like you to engage the collective in imagining a new way forward?

This competency results in how both the issue and organization is seen and understood, and it creates the tribe of people who choose to be part of the conversation.

When you excel at Influence and Enrolling, you build a movement of people actively working to transform the situation.

Every competency is named for a way of being and the outcome that is achieved when a leader stands fully in that pillar. There are interconnections between each pillar:

- **Courage** is required in all of them and is strongest in the competencies of Integrity and Courage, and Influence and Enrolling, as they result in the biggest shift (remember courage is a catalyst emotion that lies between below the line and above the line emotions) and it is often deeply difficult to stand clearly in the scrutiny of the public arena and say what you stand for and ask others to join you.
- **Commitment and connection** to your own values, beliefs, and faith are required for all four competencies because if you don't know what you stand for, you can't affect change.
- **Authenticity and humility** in equal parts are woven through all four competencies –authenticity resonates and deepens the humanity between yourself and others, and humility orients you towards growth, learning and a willingness to try and fail, and get up and begin again.

The foundations underlying the model are:

- Give yourself full permission for authenticity; and
- Take full responsibility for impact.

Reflect and Practice – You and the Courageous Leadership Model

Ask yourself:

- What are your strengths? Which of the four competencies in the Courageous Leadership Model is a strength for you?
- What skills, knowledge, and ways of being do you have in each of the four competencies?
- What are your growing edges? Which of the four competencies do you need to lean into and expand or stretch?
- What impact would it have if you lead yourself and others with access to all four competencies?

The foundations underlying the Courageous Leadership Model are 1) Leaders give themselves full permission for authenticity and 2) Leaders take responsibility for their impact.

- What does it look like when you lead authentically, showing up fully as your whole self? How is that different or similar to what you do now? What impact would it have on the conversation or situation if you showed up authentically?
- What does it mean to take responsibility for impact? How do you differentiate between intention and impact?
- What are some actions you can take to step more fully into authenticity and responsibility for impact?

Reflect on What You Have Learned

I began this book with a story about my grandfather and the depth of what I learned from him about talking together about hard things. The difference between our generations, worldviews, politics, and values were ever present. In the end, what kept us together was love and a shared commitment to relationship, to disagree well with kindness and courage. When you look to your life and work, being there for each other in all of our differences and similarities is as simple and as complex as that.

Thank you for reading.

Thank you for picking up this book and being curious enough to dream of the possibility of a world where we talk together about the things that matter most.

In the end, changing the world starts with you and with me, and the choices we each make in our lives, organizations, and communities.

One conversation at a time.

Starting today.

I'd love to hear your thoughts, reflections, and stories. If you want to share and connect, please reach out. You can find me at www.bravelylead.com

Acknowledgments

Every participant in every conversation I have led taught me something that I included in this book. Every contribution, story, passionate statement, and hard question has informed my faith in people, and our capacity to talk about anything together if we try hard enough.

I'm indebted to the memory of my grandparents, Jim and Geraldine Crate. From Gerri I learned the love of cooking for a gathering, and from Jim, the foundations of talking together with love and respect, even when we hold vastly different ways of seeing the world. A heartfelt thanks to my parents Judi and Gerry for their love, support, and cheerleading for this book.

I'm grateful to my family, friends, colleagues, and fellow leaders along the way who have encouraged me, challenged me, called me out, and helped me process the joy, challenge, and pain of this work.

I'm especially grateful to Jenn and Ian who read early drafts as I stumbled along, gave me feedback, and listened while I questioned and second-guessed myself and my ability to finish the book. Your support and insight meant this book got finished.

To Mathilda, who was my first real reader, and helped me see the web of connections and tensions that tie everything together in life – and in this book. I'm so appreciative of your wisdom and insight.

To those of you who read stories in this book to let me know if I had accurately and fairly reflected our relationship and interaction, thank you for your grace and kindness.

To my favourite people: my children. I'm grateful every day for your insights, wisdom and how humble you keep me.

To my best friend and life partner, Ian, who has always encouraged my wild ideas and my seeking the next adventure and frontier. I am forever grateful for your kindness, love, and support.

I'm so thankful for each reader of this book – together we build the world we want to live in, one brave, honest conversation at a time.

www.ingramcontent.com/pod-product-compliance
Lightning Source LLC
Chambersburg PA
CBHW061148120626
46546CB00005B/1967